Autism and Enablement

Autism and Enablement

Occupational Therapy Approaches to Promote Independence for Adults with Autism

Matt Bushell, Sandra Gasson and Ute Vann

Jessica Kingsley *Publishers*
London and Philadelphia

First published in 2018
by Jessica Kingsley Publishers
73 Collier Street
London N1 9BE, UK
and
400 Market Street, Suite 400
Philadelphia, PA 19106, USA

www.jkp.com

Library of Congress Cataloging in Publication Data
Names: Bushell, Matt, author. | Gasson, Sandra, author. | Vann, Ute, author.
Title: Autism and enablement : occupational therapy approaches to promote
   independence for adults with autism / Matt Bushell, Sandra Gasson and Ute
   Vann.
Description: London ; Philadelphia : Jessica Kingsley Publishers, 2018. |
   Includes bibliographical references and index.
Identifiers: LCCN 2017028842 | ISBN 9781785920875 (alk. paper)
Subjects: | MESH: Autism Spectrum Disorder--rehabilitation | Occupational
   Therapy--methods | Rehabilitation Research | Adult
Classification: LCC RC553.A88 | NLM WM 203.5 | DDC 616.85/88206--dc23 LC
record available at https://lccn.loc.gov/2017028842

British Library Cataloguing in Publication Data
A CIP catalogue record for this book is available from the British Library

ISBN 978 1 78592 087 5
eISBN 978 1 78450 348 2

Printed and bound in Great Britain

The term Enablement is crucial to our understanding of the needs of autistic people...[t]he emphasis being on person-led support rather than what professionals think a person might need. It is important to discuss options which can be employed by an individual to aid self-management and well-being without the need for direct support from another person. An important conclusion made [in this book] is that some people will need help and support from others at times, whilst others will need ongoing support; different support may be needed at different times. Autism is a life-long condition but it is vital that any assessment of needs is individually based and focusses on strengths and the person's well-being and self-management.

Judith Gould

Contents

Foreword

Children with autism grow up and become adults. Autism does not disappear at the age of 18. Everyone knows that. Yet, after 75 years of autism research, most interventions still aim at children and young people. Little, too little, is known about strategies for supporting adults with autism in their struggle for a happy, productive and meaningful life. *Autism and Enablement* addresses a major need of parents and professionals for useful tools and strategies to support adults with autism.

According to self-determination theory, human beings have three innate fundamental needs that, if met, enable them to grow, develop and flourish. These three needs – competence, relatedness and autonomy – are universal, and there is thus no reason to believe that people with autism do not have them. In this book, Matt Bushell, Sandra Gasson and Ute Vann present a comprehensive research and evidence-based foundation for assessing the needs of and supporting (young) adults with autism. Using occupational therapy tools for assessment, training and support, the foundation aims at enhancing the competence, autonomy and relatedness of adults with autism in a way that is unique because it takes a contextualised and bottom-up – or 'feet on the ground' – rather than a generic and top-down, approach to increasing the independence and well-being of adults with autism. The Kent ASC Team's foundation is person-centred and the support offered is based on a detailed assessment of not only an individual's needs, interests and goals in life, but also their unique living environment, including the often overlooked sensory aspects of that environment.

With its unique combination of research data and illustrative case examples, *Autism and Enablement* is a rich source of information and inspiration for everyone (not only occupational therapists but also other professionals, parents and even policy makers) looking for ways to increase the independence, relatedness and competence of young adults with autism.

Peter Vermeulen

Acknowledgements

We would like to say thank you for the assistance and support of Anna Goode and Triangle Consulting, Abigail Vincent, Gerry Harding and Sonia Stevens at Kent County Council for their technical support; Tabitha Hunter for her clinical occupational therapy support; Jenny Beecham for her valuable research advice; Charlotte Morgan, Sue Eltringham and Nikki Webster (Kent County Council) for their excellent delivery of the Enablement intervention; and the wider Kent Autistic Spectrum Conditions Team for their wider contribution. For helping to steer our research, we would like to thank the Enablement Research Focus Group members: Sarah Kean, Julie Beadle-Brown, Denise Eden-Green, Cliff Robins, Nicola Waddington, Tracy Mapp, Carol Carter and Austen Hughes. Thanks to Beryl Palmer, P. J. Hughes, Mohammed Rizwan, Judith Gould, Peter Vermeulen and Chris Barson for commenting on drafts; Lisa Clark and Sarah Hamlin of Jessica Kingsley Publishers for their patience and support, and Beryl Palmer, our manager, with Anne Tidmarsh, Director, Older Persons and Physical Disability (Kent County Council) for believing in practitioners to deliver innovation.

The authors acknowledge the support of their colleagues and of Kent County Council in allowing these research findings to be shared. The views and conclusions expressed are, however, those of the authors alone.

Introduction

Matt Bushell

Jenny, a married woman in her mid-twenties, worked in a qualified professional role before resigning after a mental health regression. She was also pregnant with her first child. Throughout her life she had struggled with a feeling of difference and found daily living tasks overly complicated and social environments overwhelming. Her mother had to visit to help with routine tasks and found herself in the role of carer rather than mother and soon-to-be grandmother. Jenny's mother cleaned the house weekly because of Jenny's aversion to the smell of bleach, amongst other issues.

Jenny was diagnosed with autism, following which the diagnostic team, with her agreement, made a referral to the Kent ASC Team. The team completed a social care assessment in accordance with the Care Act 2014, which led to her agreeing to be part of an 'ASC Enablement' trial – a 12-week provision led by a specialist occupational therapist. As part of the Enablement trial Jenny undertook sensory and motor processing assessments, which revealed the significant difficulties she experienced in daily living and functioning. These difficulties appeared to be in juxtaposition to her educational and vocational attainments. Jenny was highly motivated and took on all the advice and assistance provided, enhancing her existing strengths and learning new skills. One day during the Enablement period, Jenny texted her Enablement support worker to state that she had cleaned her whole house independently. She had done so primarily by using noise-cancelling headphones to remove one of her senses (hearing) to allow her to accommodate her aversion to the smell of cleaning products. Her advancements in overall functioning, which became increasingly efficient and within timescales set for each task, had a massive impact upon her life and well-being.

Jenny's autistic condition continues to pose daily challenges for her but she feels she is better equipped to deal with them, whilst her mother enjoys just coming round for tea.

The desire for independence is at the very heart of the human condition. The thought of asking others for support can be a frightening prospect to many and could be perceived by some as a loss of control. For someone on the autistic spectrum, this can be a particularly undesirable prospect: the very act of engaging with unfamiliar people – however kind and helpful these people might be – is often to be avoided and can be easily understood within a general understanding of the condition.

The reality, though, is that we all need support at various times in our lives; often, in the case of family support, we might rely heavily upon those family members but do not acknowledge it as *support* or envisage how things might be if that support ever ceased. Even the most independent person will on occasions need a greater level of support, perhaps during a time of significant change or during a transitional stage in their life. This situation is particularly true for people who are higher functioning on the autism spectrum who can struggle with significant change as an accepted trait of their condition. They can often be overlooked in relation to their need for support, because they may have strengths in some areas but are then assumed to have strengths in all; that if they can do 'that' task, then they can, according to normal logic, do 'these other' tasks too. Unfortunately, the situation is not that simple but this assumption can be very disabling – unnecessarily so. If Jenny had been assessed by someone in a non-specialist ASC team, it is likely that they would have dismissed her inability to manage those tasks of daily living; the assessment would have been insufficiently detailed to reveal that Jenny's motor-processing skills fell within the range of a person with a learning disability – despite the fact that she was a qualified professional.

During the past few decades a person in need of formal care and support from the state has had to agree to a 'needs' assessment. *Need* can often be a professional judgement based upon a practitioner's normalised understanding of what might be required by a person with a certain condition and within a certain support network. The assessor might complete the assessment in partnership with the individual, then rationalise with them about what support would be reasonable to provide to meet that need – along with the outcomes they hope to achieve. For instance, a young person leaving the family home for the first time might need three calls a day, equalling 21 hours inclusive per week. This would seem entirely reasonable in support of such a life-changing event (and may reduce over time as the person settles). In reality, however, such a formulaic approach might not always work well when considering ASC support because the needs of people on the spectrum are so individual. Two people, for example, could present in very similar ways and have similar support networks in place but actually require very different levels of assistance.

For this reason, during the second year of the Kent ASC team's existence, we questioned how we could extend our range of assessment and provision to better empower the clients we are charged to support to develop self-management skills and a greater feeling of well-being. We sought to develop a methodology for individually assessing the impact of a life-long autistic condition, and thereby provide support and recommendations regarding how each person could achieve their desired personal outcomes.

With few specialist adult social work teams for clients with higher-functioning autism, the Kent ASC team considered that they were well placed to consider such transformative work. What became progressively more clear as the team progressed past their thousandth client assessment, however, was that, although their specialist ASC assessment was proving highly beneficial, it did not provide a sufficient picture of a person's functional abilities within their usual contexts; that is, it did not 'unpick' why certain tasks were difficult for the person to achieve and what could mitigate such difficulties.

It was by good fortune that our team included an occupational therapy-qualified case manager/social worker who was able to trial some specialist ASC approaches using her occupational therapy skills and training. Adult services social workers in Kent have for many years worked in tandem with occupational therapists, and over the past decade have utilised Enablement interventions for other adult client groups. Occupational therapists have also worked successfully in the short term with children with autism who have a learning disability or mental health issue to promote their independence. Occupational therapists specialise in working within a person's social and occupational environments and contexts. Such an approach marries well with supporting clients with an ASC because, though a lifelong condition, individual presentations of ASC can certainly be affected by the social context of the individual and, additionally, how they interact with and relate to their social world, including in terms of their sensory preferences.

We therefore set about securing funds to trial a specialist ASC Enablement intervention, centring on occupational therapy but working in tandem with specialist ASC social workers. A two-year study was proposed, and duly accepted, twelve months of which was designated a social care research project.

This book documents our journey as we established specialist Enablement provision for clients in Kent with autism. It demonstrates how specialist professionals can enable people on the autistic spectrum to realise better lives, and provides a resource for commissioners deciding whether to invest in this cost-effective and high-impact intervention. We meet many clients who have been offered specialist help for psychological and mental health problems, and medication for such; however, there are very few localised autism teams working to limit the need for these higher-level interventions. The onus is therefore on the small number of autism teams that do exist to prove that they can deliver personalised interventions and approaches, and thereby challenge current health commissioning to invest more in preventative community services.

This book describes the background to the Kent ASC team's specialist Enablement intervention. Each chapter is written by one of the three Enablement research team members who founded the intervention, based on their individual specialisms within the project: autism practice, research and occupational therapy. Chapter 1 establishes the context of our specialist work with clients on the autistic spectrum and describes how understanding of ASCs has evolved. Chapter 2 covers why we considered it beneficial to trial a specialist Enablement intervention, considering issue-specific research, relevant literature and the views of people with autism. Chapter 3 describes the specialist Enablement intervention itself, from the perspective of the occupational therapy role. Chapter 4 details our research findings and provides individual case studies. Finally, Chapter 5 considers whether the intervention has delivered its objectives, explores the key learning to be gained from the research and our Enablement intervention.

Chapter 1

Understanding Autistic Spectrum Conditions and their Impact on the Individual

Matt Bushell

In the UK, the Autism Act 2009 and subsequent guidance (detailed in Chapter 2) called for improved services for the autistic client group, particularly for those who are higher-functioning. This is much needed in the UK, and also globally because some individuals with an autistic spectrum condition (ASC) discuss that they have been denied assistance entirely, despite appearing to be 'eligible' for both assessment and support.

Historically, a great many people on the spectrum have also found themselves floundering within the mental health systems of the world. This is no criticism of the professionals involved, however, who may have deemed mental health intervention to be in their best interest from a clinical perspective, but their issues were associated to autism and not mental health per se. As time has moved on, though, so too has our attainment of knowledge about neurodevelopmental conditions – and their distinct characteristics separate from mental health conditions (accepting of course that there is a relationship – an issue discussed further in this Chapter). Year on year appreciation of this issue is growing but there is still a severe lack of research concerning best practice in supporting those who are higher-functioning on the spectrum. Research regarding adults on the spectrum grows yearly, but between 1946 and 2011 just 23 per cent of all autism research concerned adults and most of this focused on adults with a learning disability. Even more concerning was the fact that approximately only 1 per cent of ASC research focused on older people (Mukaetova-Ladinska *et al.* 2012). We are pleased to see new books highlighting *evidence-based* best practice in autism spectrum disorders/autism spectrum conditions, such as Kenneth Aitken's (2015) evaluation of principal assessment methods; however, as our literature review evidenced (see Chapter 2), such evaluations are few and far between relative to the prevalence of the condition worldwide. There is therefore still much to do in terms of recognising and addressing neurodevelopmental need – and this book seeks in part to redress these inequities.

Today, people are increasingly offered the opportunity to gain a diagnosis later in life, affording individuals (and those who help them) a greater understanding of their lifelong difficulties. Unfortunately, those who are diagnosed late have obviously missed out on targeted support throughout the course of their life. The person's ability to achieve a sense of well-being and learn self-management skills may well have been impeded by the ability of others to recognise their needs. Also, although they no doubt have been seen by others as 'outside of the norm', the person may actually have been labelled 'abnormal' rather than be judged informed by a neurodevelopmental appreciation of *difference*. While history cannot be changed, it is important today that people on the spectrum are offered a timely assessment and post-diagnosis options, that the means to offer early diagnosis are commissioned and that an autistic diagnosis is projected not as a disabling label but as something of worth.

Autistic spectrum disorder (ASD) is a clinical term. Throughout this book, however, we take the liberty of revising it to autistic spectrum condition (ASC) – except where discussing the diagnostic category itself – because the word 'condition' is much more acceptable to those on the spectrum. 'Condition' is a *way of being*; 'disorder' has many negative connotations. ASD according to the two global classification systems (see below), is one of a number of 'disorders' within the *catch-all* category of 'mental disorder'. The identification of ASC as a mental disorder has been roundly challenged worldwide because it is increasingly now seen from the perspective of 'neurodiversity'; that is, as having links to genetics and biology and neurological origins. Although no one knows the exact cause of ASCs, there is growing awareness that early brain development and different 'wiring' in the brain are involved. The problem of classifying ASCs as mental disorders is most powerfully challenged by the viewpoint of a person with an ASC themselves. They inevitably and reasonably state: 'Who says I am disordered? My mind works differently but to say I am disordered is to insist on a level of maladaptation – that the order of my brain is wrong. If this is correct, then how come so many people with ASCs have contributed so much to modern life – to human advancement generally and, specifically, in technology, science, astrophysics...? It could be argued that, if any maladaptation does exist, it lies in the inability of those without an ASC to understand the differences associated with the condition and to accommodate them. This brings us neatly to a famous Temple Grandin (professor of animal science and autism spokesperson) mantra about autistic spectrum conditions, 'different not less', which is a great way to consider the presentation of the condition.

ASCs, together with attention deficit hyperactivity disorder (ADHD) and some other conditions, are increasingly seen as a 'neurodevelopmental' condition; that is, an impairment of the growth and development of the brain or central nervous system, which can affect, amongst other things, a person's learning ability, self-control, emotion and memory over the lifespan.

Diagnosis of autistic spectrum disorders has not evolved in a simple manner. Indeed, although many diagnostic assessment tools are available, offering varying levels of accuracy, many people remain unscreened because ASD is still very much in its infancy, clinically, relative to many other conditions. There are also, without doubt, those who are diagnosed with a mental health condition who do not actually have mental health issues but instead are on the spectrum – and vice versa. Two classification systems for diagnosing ASC/ASD are available: the World Health Organization's International Classification of Diseases (ICD) is primarily used in the UK and the *Diagnostic and Statistical Manual* (*DSM*) is used in the US. The *DSM-5* (American Psychiatric Association 2013) revises the classification of 'Autistic Spectrum Disorder'. *DSM-IV*, and earlier editions, identified five subsets within the term 'spectrum disorder', including Asperger syndrome, a condition defined by Hans Asperger in 1944. According to *DSM-5* criteria, a person would be assessed as having an ASD if they have significant problems in two domains:

1. Social communication and interaction

2. Restricted, repetitive patterns of behaviour

If restricted, repetitive behaviours are not present, the person would receive a social communication disorder (SCD) diagnosis and not a full ASD diagnosis. The UK's National Autistic Society anticipates that problems may arise if the ICD follows the *DSM-5* guidelines in its next revision, and with some justification. Neurodiversity presents so individually that some people *autistic in presentation* might have more distinct traits in the social triad (that is, impairment related to imagination, social communication and social interaction), whereas others may have more pronounced traits in their restricted and repetitive behaviour – such is the rich tapestry of autism that they are all on the spectrum. A diagnosis of a social communication disorder is not necessary and over-complicates matters, and may possibly also work to deny support to people who might overwise have obtained it with an ASD diagnosis. That said, the National Autistic Society does recognise some benefits of the *DSM-5* categorisation, in that sensory behaviours are included for the first time within the 'restricted and repetitive behaviour domain', and the emphasis has changed from 'giving a name' to a condition to identifying how much someone is affected by that condition. Both of these areas are important, in particular the former, in terms of understanding how severely a person is affected by the condition, because this is relevant to the likelihood of support being required. This is not a simple area because as stated two people can have a similar ASD presentation and yet one may never need support and the other require comprehensive support – such is the uniqueness of ASCs.

The National Autistic Society (2016) provides a useful description of autism on its website:

> [Autism is a] lifelong developmental disability that affects how a person communicates with, and relates to, other people and the world around them. Autistic Spectrum Condition affects 1 in 100 people. It is a Spectrum condition, which means that, while all people with Autism have certain difficulties, their condition will affect them in different ways. There is no known cure for Autism. Some people with Autism are able to live relatively independent lives but others may need a lifetime of specialist support. The main areas of difficulty are in recognising and understanding other people's feelings and managing their own, using and understanding verbal and non-verbal language, understanding and predicting other people's intentions and behaviour and imagining situations outside of their own routine. People with Autism may also experience over- or under-sensitivity to sounds, touch, tastes, smells, light or colours.

Supporting high-functioning autistic people

We believe that the specialist Enablement intervention adopted in our research could be utilised to support all those on the autistic spectrum. Indeed, none of the assessments are designed by us and, though some are licensed, they are all publically available. Elements of the overall approach are no doubt already used to support clients with a learning disability and children in primarily educational settings; however, during the searches we conducted for our literature review we found no approach utilising the fusion of elements adopted in our combined Enablement intervention.

Although we believe the Kent Enablement intervention could provide benefit to all those across the spectrum, we need to make clear that the intervention was trialled with participants of *higher ability/ intellect* on the autistic spectrum; the cohort that the Kent ASC team are charged with supporting. It is important to state this because, although we acknowledge specialist Enablement's wider potential benefits, some of the successes evidenced in future chapters relied on an assumption that the person's overall intellectual and processing ability was sufficient to take on the challenges of the intervention; for those with less ability, further adjustments and adaptations would no doubt have to be made.

To describe this cohort more fully, generally people considered 'higher-functioning' on the spectrum would generally have better social skills and verbal ability than those categorised as lower-functioning and possess an intellectual capacity within 'normal ranges' (Attwood 1998), such as those historically diagnosed with Asperger syndrome. Even within an Asperger syndrome cohort, however, we have observed a significant number of people who are intellectually lower-functioning than the norm but not eligible for learning disability services; these people might have spikes of intellect and ability in certain areas – such is the nature of autism.

In the past, local authorities and health trusts erroneously used a person's IQ (intelligence quotient) to determine whether they were higher- or lower-functioning. Such judgements were then used to justify people's eligibility to access services and health interventions. This method is now seen as problematic and, though there have been positive developments of late in addressing such inequities, some challenges remain. If ASCs are truly understood, judgements based upon IQ alone are unsatisfactory. Many studies investigate this issue, including that of Charman *et al.* (2011), who conclude that ASCs are not as strongly associated with intellectual disability as once thought; indeed, the IQ of a person with an ASC was less relevant than their adaptive impairment. What this means is that standard IQ tests – based upon a normative population – do not account for the nuances and individualism of an ASC. There is a difference between a learning impairment as a result of a person having a distinct learning disability and the profound impact of autism. It may be that a person's ability to learn is untapped in some areas because they have not had access to the approaches to learning that match their own intelligences. On this subject, according to the National Autistic Society (and US prevalence data is similar), it is reasonable to consider that:

44–52 per cent of people with autism may have a learning disability

48–56 per cent of people with autism do not have a learning disability

The National Autistic Society acknowledges that there is a level of variance and ambiguity here, because of methodologies and sample size, but essentially the main issue is that the ability of those with an ASC cannot be measured accurately based on IQ, and intelligence takes many forms – emotional, functional, intellectual, contextual, to name but a few. For example, a judgement of intellect will not explain how someone deemed higher-functioning and with significant verbal ability may still have significant deficits in performance/executive functioning even in relation to tasks perceived as 'basic'.

The other important point here is that people *learn* best in their everyday contexts, and many clinic-based tests are not fit for purpose. This is the area we seek to assess using the specialist ASC Enablement intervention. We work in the client's familiar context/s and then help them to transfer new skills into new contexts. We also seek to help people with autism to use their greater intellect to attain the optimum skills of independence, individual to themselves.

People higher-functioning on the spectrum often talk about the condition as a *hidden disability*, and it is a great development to see car stickers announcing 'Not all disabilities are visible' and Facebook pages named similarly. If the hidden needs of a person higher-functioning on the spectrum are not considered, then their overall life chances are severely affected; if no reasonable adaptations/ adjustments can be made in the work environment, then they may have less chance of holding down a job; if a doctor is not able to see the issues inherent in the condition, their access to essential health support can be compromised; and if teachers do not understand the ways in which they learn, then educational attainment is so much further from their grasp.

Many assumptions are made about those higher-functioning on the spectrum. For example, a common misunderstanding is that they are all 'autistic savants'; that is, experts in certain areas, such as art or science, or able to recite the names of all the American presidents. This perception is supported by the portrayal of the main character in the film *Rain Man* (1988) and by Sheldon in *The Big Bang Theory*. Dr Bernard Rimland (1978), who first coined the term autistic savant, believed that just 10 per cent of people with an ASC have savant abilities, but even then only in some areas. He speculated that this high-functioning skill results from a person's ability to focus completely on one area of interest, but often at the expense of other areas – and too often the situation can be limiting overall for the individual.

Most people would commonly consider Asperger syndrome as *the term* to define higher-functioning autism, and in many cases they are right. However, differences are felt to exist between higher-functioning autism and Asperger syndrome. Such differences concern delay in language development, self-stimulating behaviour and ability to read non-verbal clues, for example. Identifying the differences between these two definitions is a struggle, however, and maybe the fact that Asperger syndrome has been withdrawn from one of the two global diagnostic classification systems is helpful to this issue. Conversely, many people with Asperger syndrome are resentful of this development and value the term 'Aspergers' – adapting it to Aspie and Aspergic – as a means of cultural and personal identification. Being defined as someone with Asperger syndrome rather than someone with a variance of autism is perhaps preferable because Aspergers (the term we will now use throughout this book) in many ways has gained itself a certain respect in the world of conditions. The term 'autism', meanwhile, can cause some people on the spectrum to worry that it has connotations of lower-ability as in Leo Kanner's (1943) definition of classic autism – Kanner being the first to identify autism as a distinct condition. Autism is widely used in the modern era as a catch-all term and an Autism Act 2009 actually exists in the UK; however, one of the principal agendas of that Act is to mitigate gaps in service provision for people higher-functioning on the spectrum.

Recognising that some people with Asperger syndrome or higher functioning autism can present as very 'able' – and clearly are – but may still have difficulties in some areas of life is challenging for local and health authorities throughout the world. We have previously presented a case study of a person with Aspergers who, while possessing professional qualifications, nonetheless demonstrated motor/processing difficulties that would be assessed as within a range of a learning disability. We hope that this book offers something to this argument and prevents judgements and assumptions about eligibility and access to assessment and services generally – true eligibility cannot be ascertained without effective assessment.

Rosenblatt (2008, p. 6) emphasises the sorry state of affairs for people on the spectrum in the UK:

> 63% of adults with Autism do not have enough support to meet their needs; 92% of parents are worried about their son's or daughter's future when they are no longer able to care for them; 61% of adults with Autism rely on their family financially and 40% live with their parents.

The Autism Act 2009 has encouraged authorities to provide better services but there is still a long way to go in the UK. In the US, 35 per cent of those with an ASC aged 19–23 had never had a job or had not been able to continue their education (Shattuck *et al.* 2012). The risks involved in not offering support are clear: if a young person with higher-functioning autism does not have a job and leaves education *voids* will appear in their life. People on the spectrum are often looking to fill voids and gaps in their lives because structure and routine are so important. Lack of structure and routine leads some young people to regress in terms of their independence, self-management and well-being, causing extreme frustration, the opting-out of social participation and the loss of confidence and competence previously gained. It is often at this point that some people's behaviour might be considered challenging but often this is the result of not being helped to develop at a critical and formative stage of their life.

A final issue associated with those who are higher-functioning on the spectrum is that they often have good *surface* language skills.

Language and linguistics in terms of ASCs are, however, far from simple concepts, and someone may come across as an excellent linguist – and may well be – but might still have problems using language appropriate to context; that is, they may have learnt phrases that have assisted them in communication generally but which are not applicable to all contexts. One female client we encountered, who was higher-functioning on the spectrum, told us that there was an even deeper issue with language related to ASCs: language did not come naturally to her and it took her many years to learn to use it; she saw herself as principally a sensory being for whom language had little relevance in her own world. She added:

> *The thing I have found is there is not language for everything that there is, so how can one communicate it other than through using things to describe things that are close to it but are not it, because a name, phrase, etc. has not been given to it yet; there appears no common, agreed understanding.*

Considering ASCs and co-existing conditions

People with an ASC diagnosis often also have other conditions. During the course of our intervention, there were differences in success rates between those with autism alone, and those with autism compounded by a co-existing condition/s. Although samples were small, people with autism alone were the most successful, followed by people with autism and ADHD coexisting. Those with ADHD not treated with medication or those with mental health issues co-existing provided greater challenges for both themselves and the Enablement team; although they still displayed improvements overall.

Recommendations to assist people on the spectrum in their overall independence and well-being, such as those in our Enablement intervention, should therefore consider any co-existing condition, additional to autism. The National Autistic Society states that 70 per cent of people with an ASC will have one co-existing condition and 50 per cent will have two other conditions.

Seventy per cent of people will have some kind of learning difficulty it is stated, but is this really so? Probably, and particularly so if we consider that 50 per cent of people on the spectrum are considered to have a learning disability diagnosis. The learning difficulties of people higher-functioning on the spectrum may be more subtle though, and influenced by additional conditions such as dyslexia or apraxia. A US study (Tierney *et al.* 2015) found that apraxia (difficulty with coordinating the tongue, lips, mouth and jaw in order to produce speech) was present in 64 per cent of the children with an ASC sampled – though it must be noted that the sample involved all people on the spectrum not just children higher-functioning on the spectrum. Possibly, however, if people higher-functioning on the spectrum were diagnosed earlier and received school teaching targeted to their strengths fewer would possibly be deemed to have a learning difficulty. Indeed, given sufficient social, health and educational support, at the right time, some higher-functioning students could be seen to have a *learning advantage*, that is, their strengths might well be maximised, such as attention to detail, ability to focus, desire to complete tasks and so on.

The nexus between mental health and ASCs is, like most areas of ASC analysis, a complicated affair. Three areas of association exist:

- Those people with a co-existing ASC and mental health diagnosis; for example, 10 per cent of people with an ASC also have obsessive compulsive disorder (OCD).

- Those people whose ASC traits have regressed to the extent that they have developed significant mental health problems. They might also have ADHD or severe attachment issues compounding their overall presentation.

- Those people with an ASC who are seen as having some 'mental health traits' that are in fact ASC traits; that is, moderate to severe levels of depression, anxiety, feelings of hopelessness to the point of expressed suicidal ideation, and compulsive or obsessive behaviours.

People with an ASC are sometimes diagnosed with OCD or psychosis, or as experiencing hallucinations or hearing voices, when these can sometimes be extended traits of ASCs and not co-existing conditions at all. A good example is someone stating that they are 'hearing voices' when in fact they are 'hearing' their own thoughts and not a *psychotic* 'other' voice – a voice of reason or echolalia (meaningless repetition of words spoken by someone else) or repeating advice or articulating a fantasy. Such behaviour could result from the mixing up of senses – even synaesthesia – that is sometimes present as a feature of ASCs.

As previously stated, mental health treatments and anti-psychotic medication have historically been offered as a means of 'treating' the more severe ASC traits; and some clients with long-term exposure to such are at risk of Tardive dyskinesia (involuntary, repetitive body movements), which in itself could be missed if seen instead by professionals as traits, anxiety systems or 'stimming' (self-stimulating) behaviour. It is with this history in mind that autism guidance in the UK and US increasingly calls for psycho-educational or social solutions to be trialled before considering medication. Our specialist Enablement intervention offers such a social solution, exploring the individual causes of issues that impact those with an ASC in a 'bottom-up approach' (detailed in Chapter 3).

The National Autistic Society states that 30 per cent of people with an ASC will also have ADHD, and we have seen a similar ratio within our team. ADHD is understood within its own triad of social impairments: inattentiveness, hyperactivity and impulsiveness. There are many similarities between these two conditions. Similarities relate to mood, anxiety, language issues, socialisation, planning and executive functioning, risk-taking, understanding others, emotional regulation, memory and recall, focus and change. Diane Kennedy (2002) researched the linkages between ASCs and ADHD because her three sons were diagnosed with such. She felt that there were elements of diagnostic confusion in relation to the two conditions. She identified many behaviours that were equally common in both conditions, a situation similar to the links between dyspraxia and other neurodevelopmental conditions. For example, the three main issues of impulsivity, hyperactivity and inattention associated with ADHD could also be observed in some people with a single diagnosis of ASC. However, the apparent inattention of a person with an ASC might simply result from their lack of interest in the task at hand and/or inability to see its significance, rather than an inability to focus per se; people with an ASC are, of course, very good at focusing, in context and on a particular object or subject of interest. ASC 'traits' are also seen in, or co-exist with, conditions such as Fragile X or Tourette's syndrome because these conditions, like ADHD, are neurodevelopmentally determined (Frith 2006), and in many ways cannot be seen as separate from ASCs in those individuals who are affected as they combine and interact with each other.

Physical health issues are also underestimated in those with ASCs. Diabetes and epilepsy are among the co-existing health conditions which might co-present. The self-management of such conditions can sometimes be a challenge and specialist Enablement interventions, though not specifically designed to manage health problems, can often help. Physical issues can sometimes develop as a consequence of ASC traits, such as chronic back pain or orthodontic issues as a result of grinding teeth/avoiding the dentist. Another area very much under-acknowledged is the co-existence of gastro-intestinal problems in those with an ASC (i.e. diarrhoea, abdominal pain, constipation). Virginia Bovell (2014) researched this issue extensively and discovered a prevalence rate of 9–91 per cent in varying studies explored. She makes an interesting point in questioning whether some 'challenging behaviours' in ASC are in fact 'pain' behaviours. Whether anxiety also plays a part in gastro-intestinal issues generally for people on the spectrum also remains a question to be addressed.

Research conducted by Croen *et al.* (2015) in the US revealed that adults on the spectrum also have a greater likelihood than people in the general population of experiencing problems with immune conditions, obesity, dyslipidaemia (an abnormal amount of lipids in the blood) and hypertension. As regards obesity, there are a number of reasons why this can be a risk for people with autism, including poor self-esteem and sensory issues such as an inability to feel sated. Both men and women with ASCs can experience weight and self-image issues. Baron-Cohen (2013) states that anorexia and autism have many common features – a fascination for detail, a tendency to focus on oneself, inflexible behaviours and rigid attitudes – and also share similar changes in the structure and function of particular regions of the brain. Although both men and women with an ASC can develop anorexia, women are considered to be generally more at risk as a result of a desire to 'fit in' compounded by the influence of social media – just as in the general population.

As a social care team taking new referrals for adults, we have found that over 70 per cent of our clients are aged 17–25 years. Many of these young people have a plethora of diagnoses resulting from childhood assessments; indeed, we encountered a pleasant young man who had been diagnosed with 13 different disorders during his childhood. This situation begs the question, 'are we trying too hard to pathologise difference?' There is no easy answer to this question but as professionals we must always consider the negative impact on the individual of being labelled with a particular condition.

Recognising the different needs of females on the spectrum

Our specialist Enablement intervention has really helped us to think about the different needs of females on the spectrum. There is a growing body of research on this issue, and, in terms of diagnostic assessment, it is generally acknowledged that under-recognition is a significant problem. Currently, diagnostic tools are suspected to be male-biased, just as autism is sometimes seen as an extreme extension of male traits, that is, social awkwardness, difficulty projecting emotions and poor communication skills. It is suspected that girls and women are overlooked and underdiagnosed because they often appear passive, avoidant and hypoactive (so do not always come to the attention of professionals); have greater verbal communication skills than males (leading to superficially better social skills); and are less violent (leading to low rates of clinical referral) (Kopp 2011). In a recent US study investigating whether people on the spectrum are able to sustain further education or employment – that is, positive structured activity after mandatory schooling – Taylor, Henninger, and Mailick (2015) found that women performed significantly better than men. The explanation is thought to be that women try so much harder to adapt and conform.

Women on the spectrum can watch and study others, sometimes to the extent that it borders on a special interest. They practise and tolerate social engagement, hugs, eyes contact and so on but sometimes at a cost. Women on the spectrum can develop extreme anxiety or depression as a result of the strain, as well as high blood pressure and other health-related issues, such as anorexia, eating disorders and self-harming as desperate means of *coping*. This is not to say that males do not feel these same pressures, but women are considered to be at higher risk because, as they are less likely to be diagnosed, they are less likely to receive support.

Females are excellent at modelling, mimicking and role-playing – especially in societies in which young girls are nurtured to assume distinct female roles. Because they learn the norms and rules of these female roles, they can mask their autism more easily. Gender equality and the countering of stereotypes has progressed only so far, and girls are still bought dolls and miniature vacuum cleaners. Society enforces typical gender roles (via cartoon characters, toys, even emojis) but sometimes people with an ASC do not feel they fit into the gender or sexual role in which they find themselves. We see a great many young people seeking medical help to change gender – in both directions. Sexual diversity and gender identity are complicated issues in ASC and a subject handled superbly by Henault (2006).

The issue of 'masking' is probably the greatest double-edged sword in ASC because, although the strategy helps females to function socially, it is also disabling in its own right. The 'Autism in Pink' study (Mills and Kenyon 2013) also found that higher-functioning women will often be misjudged by others, deemed ineligible for services or not diagnosed at all because they use masking strategies to suppress their autistic traits in order to appear normal. The strategy does not always work and may instead negatively affect emotional well-being and also cause others to misjudge the person. We have often met women on the spectrum who have described having a bunch of scripts that work well for them within a number of social contexts but sometimes using them in the wrong situation; for a young woman trying to fit into a social group, this can draw unwanted and negative attention.

Zosia Zak (2006, p. 301) adds to this discussion regarding the perception of men and women on the spectrum, and describes why women have to try so hard:

> Men and women are judged differently when it comes to appearance … Men who appear grungy, archaic in their fashion sense, or just eccentric are usually excused for this shortcoming… But a grungy, unkempt, or strange-looking woman is a spectacle.

Rudy Simone (2010, p. 38) also writes extensively on the subject of females with Aspergers and relationships. She provides this insight into control issues:

> Your Aspergian darling will take 'control freak' to a fine art. This is pretty understandable once you realize that anxiety is the platform from which she operates. Control is her way of bringing safety and sensory comfort to an unpredictable, unsafe, uncomfortable world. She is also very particular about what stimuli gets into her brain.

Perhaps you have fights about the temperature in the car that have nearly come to blows, or have duelled over what program to watch on the television. Maybe she will literally scream at times if she doesn't get her way. Spoiled brat? Probably not, she probably just came that way, straight out of the box, no assembly required.

The key areas here, in terms of independence, well-being and self-management, are to ensure that women have a fair chance of being diagnosed and, once diagnosed, that their needs are not underestimated because they employ the compensatory strategies described above. It takes specialist teams and specialist approaches to identify and remedy these problems, we feel.

Females also have slightly different needs related to being at risk of manipulation by others. Robyn Steward's (2014) book, *The Independent Woman's Handbook for Super Safe Living on the Autistic Spectrum*, is a very useful resource when working in this area. It may even be that the advanced skills of females in mimicry and imitation can be augmented to enable that of greater independence, greater, that is, than males. This may account for the high number of females in our specialist Enablement cohort.

Exploring the link between the theory and impact of ASCs

Kentish psychiatrist Lorna Wing, together with Judith Gould (1979), suggested that 'autism', as a condition, presented in a number of ways best considered in terms of a 'spectrum'. Wing and Gould used the concept of a spectrum rather than a 'continuum' because it is not a condition for which people can be classified *least* to *most* severe; all kinds of combinations are possible. Some schools of thought even suggest that we are *all on the spectrum*, that traits of autism are seen in all people and that people we consider to be autistic are 'those who lie on the extreme points of personality spectra upon which we all sit' (Aitken 2017). This is probably a more valid viewpoint than the historic understanding of autism as a rare condition categorically distinct from normal development. However autism is considered, the key issue is not to dismiss those in true need, including not offering them a diagnosis. This point is supported by Luke Jackson (2002, p. 39), in relation to his own experience of school as an autistic child, who states: 'In some ways all teachers need to know [is] that a child has problems in certain areas. After all, if they don't know, they can't help.'

Kanner's definition of autism is generally thought to describe lower-functioning individuals; it is sometimes described as 'childhood autism'. Asperger syndrome, meanwhile, is seen as describing higher-functioning individuals, though perhaps more able than Hans Asperger originally proposed. Nothing is clear-cut in autism; each individual is different and has their own strengths and weaknesses. People with an ASC do, however, share characteristic traits, although the individual presentation of these traits will be highly personal to them.

When Wing and Gould proposed the concept of the spectrum, they also coined the term the 'Triad of Social Impairment' to describe the three main areas of social impairment experienced by those with an ASC:

Social communication – problems using and understanding verbal and non-verbal language, such as gestures, facial expressions and tone of voice.

Social interaction – problems recognising and understanding other people's feelings and managing their own.

Social imagination – problems understanding and predicting other people's intentions and behaviour, and imagining and understanding situations outside of their own routine.

Those with an ASC also have a tendency to engage in *narrow, repetitive patterns of activity*. In combination, these impairments can cause wider difficulties associated with feelings, thoughts, behaviour, emotions, sensory integration, language, mood, nutrition, movement, posture and attention levels. As such, Judith Gould (2008) states – and this is an important consideration within our Enablement intervention – that *everyone* with an autistic spectrum disorder diagnosis would be expected to experience some level of difficulty in coping with everyday life; specifically:

1. All will have difficulties following subtle, unwritten rules that govern social life.

2. All need other people to communicate with them in clear and easily understandable terms.

3. All are helped if complex, shifting ideas are explained in concrete terms, for example with visual illustrations.

4. All have difficulty comprehending the passage of time.

5. All have, to varying degrees, difficulty working out the consequences of their own and other people's actions

6. All need more time to process information than most other people.

7. All need to be informed of plans in advance, in clear language, and to be given careful explanations if those plans change.

8. Most experience over-sensitivity to various types of sensory input.

We have certainly witnessed these difficulties in the course of our Enablement intervention. The following chapters explain how we apply a strength-based approach to help people self-manage these difficulties.

Finally, before we conclude this chapter, it is worth briefly discussing how social work theory links to our work. Accepting the traditional understanding of autism, in relation to the social triad and rigid/repetitive behaviours, when the Kent ASC team was established in 2012 we were taught by Judith Gould that *poor* executive functioning, *lack of* central coherence and *reduced* theory of mind were key components of an overall autistic presentation. Each person presents differently, of course.

Executive function refers to a person's typical, natural ability to mentally plan, organise, remember, resolve and so on. People on the spectrum might demonstrate levels of *executive dysfunction* relating to organisation, flexibility, attention and so on. Essentially, executive dysfunction refers to an impaired ability to regulate and control thoughts and actions. This is a key area in our Enablement intervention.

Central coherence refers to the typical natural ability to make meaning from a mass of stimuli and detail. Uta Frith (1989) saw that people on the autistic spectrum demonstrated weak central coherence – they often saw the finer detail rather than the whole picture. Frith saw that this trait had both positive and negative outcomes for people with autism; for example, a benefit is that they may excel at tasks which require an attention to fine detail.

Theory of mind refers to the typical natural ability to read the intentions and thoughts of others. Simon Baron-Cohen (1995) discusses the issue of all people on the autistic spectrum being 'blind' to the mental states of others, to varying degrees, rendering them impaired in understanding what others are thinking, believing, needing and intending.

These three areas together represent the 'cognitive account' of autism, and, though sometimes challenged, many of the difficulties our clients recall can be seen as related to them. In our practice, however, it soon became clear that this was not the end of the story – implicit and explicit mentalisation were also discovered to be important. Implicit mentalisation is the fast, unconscious processing of other people's mental states; explicit mentalisation is a more conscious process whereby a person might think through *why someone said something* or acted in a certain way. If we accept that a person with an autistic condition takes time to process information, then their ability to think, make decisions and read the intentions of others 'in the moment' will be impaired; this is particularly so in situations where the information available to them is indirect or unclear. Neurotypical people can often make implicit mental decisions instantly, requiring, arguably, both conscious and subconscious processing, such is the mental agility inherent in the task; they perceive quickly and filter out instantly what is not necessary. Often our higher-ability ASC clients are better at explicit mentalisation, in the form of rumination and over-analysis – sometimes to their own detriment.

A proportion of our clients, some of whom are actually more intellectually capable than average, are able to compensate for their poor implicit mentalisation skills by explicitly reviewing a previous experience and seeking to learn from it. People with autism are often said to have greater strengths in systemising; that is, 'working out' systematically what others have gathered implicitly (Baron-Cohen 2009). We have built on this strength in our Enablement provision. We do so, conscious of the fact that a person might learn from a previous experience and apply the appropriate response/behaviour next time they find themselves in a similar situation but then find that the 'context' has changed. What worked in the previous context does not work in this new context. This draws us to another important element of autism, which, together with sensory sensitivity, has a profound impact on those with the condition: context blindness.

Dr Peter Vermeulen (2012) coined the term 'context blindness' and suggested that neurotypical people are able to make instantaneous decisions – at a speed upwards of 1/200th second – because they have an inbuilt understanding of context; a trait that is often reduced in people with autism. Vermeulen acknowledges that his work builds on that of others, particularly of Uta Frith, who saw central coherence deficits in ASC/ASD as very much linked to the effect of context on meaning.

Vermeulen's work on context has had a profound effect on the Kent ASC Team and our Enablement intervention, increasing our appreciation of the impact of ASC upon the clients we are charged to support. When clients tell their stories, it becomes apparent that so many issues link to difficulties with context, particularly in people's social engagements but also in relation to language, perception and knowledge. We have trialled a number of social skills approaches which have been useful to an extent but have not been the complete article; we now realise that we are often encouraging people with autism to learn skills in a defined context. Social life, however, is rarely defined and predictable; real life is fluid and often unpredictable. Context sensitivity is fundamental to an understanding of a person with autism's condition and its impact; even our bread and butter of *sensory assessment* is context-linked because, as Vermeulen (2012, p. 74) states:

> To process stimuli efficiently and quickly the human brain has become context sensitive... In people with autism sometimes the brain connections do not work well. The brain 'concerto' consists of fine musicians who do not play well together. The result is that stimuli are processed much more absolutely than relatively. This leads to problems including sensory challenges.

Our Enablement intervention drew on the theories discussed in this chapter, and also upon a wider understanding of sensory issues, to recognise that what we needed to do was help people with autism to be *at one* with themselves in a sensory and adaptive sense. Our specialist Enablement intervention became the team's main armoury to assist in these two areas and its evolution is described in Chapter 2.

Bibliography

Aitken, K. (2015) *Evidenced-Based Assessment Tools in ASD*. London: Jessica Kingsley Publishers, Ebook.

Aitken, P. (2017) 'Everyone is on the spectrum.' *OT Magazine* 16, May/June.

American Psychiatric Association (2013) *Diagnostic and Statistical Manual of Mental Disorders*, fifth edition. Washington, DC: American Psychiatric Association.

Attwood, T. (1998) *Asperger's Syndrome: A Guide for Parents and Professionals*. London: Jessica Kingsley Publishers, pp. 24–27.

Baron-Cohen, S., Jaffa, T., Davies, S., Auyeung, B. *et al.* (2013) 'Do girls with anorexia nervosa have elevated autistic traits?' Accessed on 27/04/2017 at www.molecularautism. biomedcentral.com/articles/10.1186/2040-2392-4-24.

Baron-Cohen, S. (1995) *Mindblindness: An Essay on Autism and Theory of Mind*. Cambridge, MA and London: MIT Press.

Baron-Cohen, S. (2009) 'Autism: The empathizing–systemizing (E–S) theory.' *The Year in Cognitive Neuroscience 2009*. Accessed on 12/05/2017 at https://pdfs.semanticscholar. org/0b31/e17725948eb4233bc8e05d2299348b40e940.pdf.

Bovell, V. (2014) 'Exploring the link between autism and gastrointestinal issues.' Presented at the National Autistic Society Professional Conference, Harrogate.

Cendrowski, M. (dir.) (n.d.) *The Big Bang Theory*. Warner Bros.

Centers for Disease Control and Prevention (2014) '1 in 68 children has been identified with autism spectrum disorder.' Accessed on 27/04/2017 at www.cdc.gov/media/ releases/2014/p0327-autism-spectrum-disorder.html.

Charman, T., Pickles, A., Simonoff, E., Chandler, S. *et al.* (2011) 'IQ in children with autism spectrum disorders: Data from the Special Needs and Autism Project (SNAP).' *Psychological Medicine* 41, 3, 619–627.

Croen, L., Zerbo, O., Qian, Y., Massolo, M. *et al.* (2015) 'The health status of adults on the autistic spectrum.' Accessed on 27/04/2017 at www.ncbi.nlm.nih.gov/pubmed/ 25911091.

Frith, C. and Frith, U. (2006) 'How we predict what other people are going to do.' *Brain Research* 1079, 36–46.

Frith, U. (1989) *Autism: Explaining the Enigma*. Oxford: Wiley-Blackwell.

Gould, J. (2008) 'The triad of impairments past, present and future.' Accessed on 02/06/2017 at http://slideplayer.com/slide/2583407.

Grandin, T. (2006) *Thinking in Pictures*. London: Bloomsbury.

Grandin, T. (2012) *Different ... Not Less: Inspiring Stories of Achievement and Successful Employment from Adults with Autism, Asperger's and ADHD*. Arlington, TX: Future Horizons.

Henault, I. (2006) *Aspergers Syndrome and Sexuality*. London: Jessica Kingsley Publishers.

Jackson, L. (2002) *Freaks, Geeks and Aspergers Syndrome*. London: Jessica Kingsley Publishing, p. 39.

Kanner, L. (1943). 'Autistic disturbances of affective contact.' *Nervous Child* 2, 217–250.

Kennedy, D. (2002) *The ADHD–Autism Connection: A Step Toward More Accurate Diagnoses and Effective Treatments*. Colorado Springs, CO: Waterbrook Press.

Kopp, S. (2011) 'Autism conditions in girls: Clinical perspectives on diagnosis, assessment and intervention.' Accessed on 07/08/2017 at www.taniamarshall.com/files/S-Kopp-Autistic-conditions-in-girls-Clinical-perspectives-on-diagnosis-assessment-and-intervention.pdf.

Levinson, B. (dir.) (1998) *Rain Man*. United Artists.

Mandy, W., Steward, R., Pinto, T., Kenyon, S. *et al.* (2014) 'Understanding women with autism.' Accessed on 25/05/2017 at www.luton.gov.uk/Health_and_social_care/ Lists/LutonDocuments/PDF/Health/Understanding%20Women%20with%20 Autism%20-%20total%20presentations.pdf.

Mills, R. and Kenyon, S. (2013) 'Prevalence study of females with autism in the four participating countries.' Accessed on 11/05/2017 at http://autisminpink.net.

Mukaetova-Ladinska, E., Perry, E., Baron, M. and Povey, C. (2012) 'Ageing in people with autistic spectrum disorder.' Accessed on 27/04/2017 at www.ncbi.nlm.nih. gov/pubmed/21538534.

National Autistic Society (2016) 'What is autism?' Accessed on 06/08/2017 at www. autism.org.uk.

Rimland, B. (1978) 'Savant capabilities of autistic children and their cognitive implications.' In G. Serban (ed.), *Cognitive Defects in the Development of Mental Illness.* New York: Brunner/Mazel.

Rosenblatt, M. (2008) *I Exist: The Message from Adults with Autism in England.* London: National Autistic Society.

Shattuck, R., Narendorf, S., Cooper, B., Sterzing, P. *et al.* (2012) 'Postsecondary education and employment among youth with an autism spectrum disorder.' Accessed on 27/04/2017 at www.pediatrics.aappublications.org/content/early/2012/05/09/ peds.2011-2864.

Simone, R. (2010) *Aspergirls: Empowering Females with Asperger's Syndrome.* London: Jessica Kingsley Publishers, p. 38.

Steward, R. (2014) *The Independent Woman's Handbook for Super Safe Living on the Autistic Spectrum.* London: Jessica Kingsley Publishers.

Taylor, J., Henninger, N., and Mailick, M. (2015) 'Longitudinal patterns of employment and post-secondary education for adults with autism and average-range IQ.' *Autism* 19, 7, 785–793.

Tierney, C., Mayes, S., Lohs, S., Black, A. *et al.* (2105) 'How valid is the checklist for autism spectrum disorder when a child has apraxia of speech?' *Journal of Developmental and Behavioral Pediatrics* 36, 8, 569–574.

Vermeulen, P. (2012) *Autism as Context Blindness.* Shawnee Mission, KS: AAPC, p. 74.

Wing, L. and Gould, J. (1979) 'Severe impairments of social interaction and associated abnormalities in children: Epidemiology and classification.' *Journal of Autism and Developmental Disorders*, 9, 11–29.

Zak, Z. (2006) *Life and Love: Positive Strategies for Autistic Adults.* Lenexa, KS: AAPC Publishing.

Chapter 2

Identifying the Need for an Enablement Intervention

Ute Vann

This chapter describes the policy contexts that led to the establishment of Kent County Council's Autistic Spectrum Conditions team and how, subsequently, the specialist Enablement research project was conceived. It includes a literature review and the research methodology.

The Kent specialist Enablement research project is set within the policy context of autism legislation and subsequent specialist services being developed by local authorities as part of adult services and the overall legal framework of the Care Act 2014. The research project was developed within Kent County Council's Autism Services, which was established in November 2012 and works with adults aged 18 and over with high-functioning autism (including Asperger syndrome).

The pre-2009 policy context

Before the Autism Act 2009 came into effect there were no national or local policies specifically and exclusively directed at the needs of adults on the autistic spectrum in the UK. Instead, their needs were included and, it could be argued, somewhat subsumed into policies for vulnerable and disabled people in general. Relevant key policies include:

> *Fair Access to Care (2002)* setting out an assessment framework and specifying how social services should identify eligibility for social care. Eligibility was graded in four bands, defined by the risk posed to someone's independence if their needs were not met.

> *Valuing People (2001)* focusing on people with learning disabilities in order to promote their rights, independence, choices and

inclusion. It was intended to enable people with learning disabilities to have control over their lives and to make choices in areas such as health, housing, employment and support for carers.

National Framework for Mental Health (2004) setting out seven national standards aimed at promoting mental health, tackling social exclusion and improving primary mental health services and joint working between health and social care agencies.

Improving the Life Chances of Disabled People (2005) focusing on promoting disabled people having full opportunities to improve their quality of life.

National Framework for Long Term Conditions (2005) setting out the quality requirements necessary to change the way in which services for people with long-term neurological conditions are provided to ensure they can live as independently as possible. This applies to health and social care and includes housing, transport, education and employment.

Our Health, Our Care, Our Say (2006) promoting more choice for people with complex needs regarding provision and control over their lives by shifting care and support closer to home and promoting Enablement and direct payments. It also promotes joint working between health and social care.

Putting People First: A Shared Vision and Commitment to the Transformation of Adult Social Care (2007) promoting the key elements of personalisation, early intervention and re-Enablement, prevention and advice, information and advocacy.

Valuing People Now (2009) restating the principles of *Valuing People (2001)* and setting out a delivery plan for the following three years.

Local policy initiatives

In line with these national policies and strategies, Kent County Council also set targets and objectives within local strategies such as Vision for Kent (2006), Towards 2010 (2006) and Active Lives (2007).

One local autism-specific policy, the Autism Policy Framework (2005), aimed at raising the educational achievement of children and young people with autism in Kent. It set out Kent County Council's expectations, including that data on children with autism should be collated, staff should have autism-specific training, adjustments should be made to school environments and named special educational needs coordinators (SENCOs) should be available to guide staff, thus ensuring smooth transition for children and young people in service provision and collaboration between health and social care.

In 2008, Kent County Council acknowledged that there appeared to be a wide range of issues and problems concerning provision for those with autism. These concerns were shared at national level and the government at the time appointed a specialist advisor for autism. In Kent, a select committee carried out a wide-ranging enquiry into the mechanisms and services provided for people with autism in the county and whether they met their needs. The brief also included recommendations for an approach to be applied in Kent. Professionals from a range of agencies, carers and support organisations contributed to this enquiry. The results were published in the *Autistic Spectrum Disorder Select Committee Report* (Kent County Council 2009). Key findings included:

- A gap between mental health and learning disabilities services. Many local authorities, including Kent County Council, organised their services to match discrete client groups with particular eligibility criteria. This meant that, for example, many adults with autism were passed between teams dealing with either their mental health or their learning disability. This chimed with a National Autistic Society report stating that many adults fall through the gap, particularly adults with high-functioning autism who do not receive any support. It also pointed out that the ASD condition is complex and that many high-functioning people with ASD still experience significant difficulties with activities of daily living and thus need support (Rosenblatt 2008).

- Lack of autism awareness in community care teams.

- Issues around transition whereby carers and clients found it difficult to access information. There was a general lack of information on service provision and transition planning did not occur in a timely manner. The process of transition was not seamless and coordinated, and continuity of service provision from children/adolescence services to adult services was problematic.

- Gaps in areas of support and the need for more services, identified by both clients and carers. The most desired support was social skills training, followed by the provision of social groups and employment support. Other support services identified were related to daily living, advocacy, befriending, day services, counselling and education.

The report recommended that Kent County Council review existing services and plan and commission future services for this client group, based on a county-wide study of incidence rates of adults with autism in need of support and not receiving it. It also stated that it should include autism-related services in care pathways provided by multi-disciplinary mental health services in the county and 'explore the possibility of setting up, in partnership with the National Health Service, a highly specialised autism service in Kent'.

National autism policy and the social care legislative framework

The Autism Act 2009 was the first legislation aimed at the needs of one specific group of disabled people. It sets out the government's commitment to improving inclusion and ensuring that adults with autism are able to participate in society, and specifically required the development of a national strategy for adults with autism.

This strategy, titled *Fulfilling and Rewarding Lives: The Strategy for Adults with Autism in England* (Department of Health 2010), identifies particular areas for action by public services based on the identified needs of people on the autistic spectrum, in particular for such people to access mainstream public services and to be included within society. The strategy speaks of encouraging 'a culture of innovation in terms of service development and delivery'. Many of the particular actions called for had also been identified during the Select Committee Enquiry, including the need for awareness raising, clear diagnostic pathways, needs assessments for adults with autism in order to identify the support they need, helping such adults into employment, local partners to plan and develop appropriate support services thus allowing them to live independently within communities, and improving processes such as transition planning. It also asked for reasonable adjustments to be made by services working with people with autism, from physical environments to service delivery.

The *Autism Self-Assessment 2011* (Roberts *et al.* 2011) assessed local authority progress in implementing the National Strategy (3 per cent of local authorities responded to a survey). Some of the overarching themes were lack of data on numbers and needs of people with autism and concern about identifying and meeting the needs of people with high-functioning autism as they were unlikely to meet eligibility criteria for social care services.

'Think Autism': An Update to the Government Adult Autism Strategy (Department of Health 2014a) then set out 15 new priority areas whilst reaffirming the importance of the areas for action identified in the strategy aimed at improving the lives of adults with autism. The 15 priorities see people with autism being part of their communities; getting the right support at the right time during their lifetime; being able to develop their skills and independence; and being able to work to the best of their ability.

Overall, Kent Adult Services, including the Kent ASC team, operate within the legal framework of the Care Act 2014. This Act reformed social care and changed the way in which people can plan and pay for their care and support. It puts a duty on local authorities to provide or arrange services that help prevent people developing needs for care and support or delay people deteriorating so that they need ongoing care and support. Other new statutory requirements enjoin local authorities to provide advocates to people who need them as part of the assessment and planning of services, and to provide support for eligible carers.

The Care Act also addresses the issue of transition from children's to adult services: local authorities are required to identify young people who are not receiving children's services but who are likely to have care and support needs as an adult. The Care Act statutory guidance specifically references young people with autism whose needs have been largely met within education services.

Establishment of the Kent ASC Team

In response to legislation and national strategic developments as well as the findings of the Kent Select Committee Enquiry, the ASC Team was created in October 2012 as a joint enterprise between social care and health, with health being responsible for diagnostic assessments. The ASC Team, providing the social care element, then began its work as a distinct specialist team for people with high-functioning autism. By 2015 the team had assessed/supported over 700 clients. A review of the first year of service operation in the Kent Adult ASC Team found a significant range of *hidden* need, including adults who in preceding years had not been able to access a social care assessment. It also highlighted the complex needs of this client group and the difficulty of being accepted by other services such as mental health, where there were significant co-existing conditions. The second-year review saw an increase in numbers of referrals for assessment and an increase in complexity of need. Kent County Council consequently recognised that the ASC Team was likely to experience continuing and increasing demand within its third year, which would be hard to accommodate without significant investment, and the team subsequently grew to a current complement of 16 staff.

The ASC Team was set up to provide community care assessments, short-term interventions, longer-term support planning, and information, advice and guidance to adults 18 years and over with autism, including Asperger syndrome, but without learning disabilities. Valios (2011) makes the case for a specialist autism team in community care provision because there is a need for specialist assessments that can identify the very specific needs arising from autism and its impact on everyday life and that assessors need specialist skills to enable them to unpick what the service user tells them.

Promoting the independence of adults with support needs through preventative and early intervention is at the heart of Kent adult social services philosophy for care and support. Such an approach can produce better outcomes for individuals and more efficient use of resources. This is particularly the case for individuals on the autistic spectrum by targeting the right support at the right people at the right time and providing person-centred responses focused on assisting individuals to self-manage rather than 'doing for' them.

Specialist needs assessments and Enablement

At its inception the service did not include provision of occupational therapy-type support such as Enablement, which is provided by Kent County Council through local adult services. As the team began its work with individuals with an ASD, knowledge about its clients grew and it became clear that assessments needed to be more specialist and include and make reference to specific areas where autism had a significant impact on people's lives. Autism affects how a person communicates with and relates to other people. It also affects how they make sense of the world around them. According to Rosenblatt (2008), without the support that an accurate and specialist assessment can lead to, many adults with an ASD may become socially isolated, drop out of college and/or suffer mental health problems or psychological breakdown that then requires expensive mental health intervention. Bancroft *et al.* (2012), three years on from the first strategy for adults with autism in England, report a clear demand from adults with autism for what could be described as 'preventative services' such as help with social skills.

What was missing was an assessment and provision of specialist support for people with autism to address sensory, functional/adaptive and socio-psychological difficulties. Such an approach would seek to address the core deficits of autism and the impact upon the individual, promote true independence, build on strengths and prevent or reduce the need for long-term packages of support. Occupational therapy provides the expertise in these areas. The National Institute for Health and Care Excellence guidelines (NICE 2012) recommend that occupational therapists be an integral part of multi-disciplinary autism services to provide specialist functional interventions. Occupational therapists have expertise in the social, emotional and physiological effects of disability and have an important role to play in providing specialist Enablement interventions for people with autism.

Enablement interventions are the cornerstone of Kent County Council's preventative initiatives with the clear intention of improving outcomes for vulnerable people. Enablement is an intensive, short-term, targeted intervention that assists individuals to regain, maintain or develop daily living skills and the confidence to carry these out to the best of their ability. As such, Enablement describes the approach that underpins all support or activities that promote independence.

General Enablement has been a core offer in Kent County Council adult services since 2009, providing time-limited intervention of up to three weeks' duration, with the option of extension by another three weeks. In mental health and learning disability services, Enablement can be provided for a period of up to 12 weeks.

Enablement is seen as providing a range of benefits for individuals, carers and Kent County Council as a local authority:

For the individual, the Enablement intervention results in:

- Increased self-esteem, the consequence of greater levels of independence.

- An increased ability to mitigate assessed areas of need, the impact of which limit the individual.

- Increased ability to cope with everyday demands and changes over context.

- Reduction or elimination of dependence upon ongoing support.

For carers:

- Reduced stress linked to their caring role.

- More time to pursue own interests or activities.

- Enhanced quality of life.

For Kent adult social services:

- A return on investment. Current evidence shows that, whilst initially Enablement is a more expensive programme compared with a domiciliary service, over a period of time individuals experience an enhanced quality of life and better outcomes and ultimately require less support.

- Reduced need to fund high-cost packages of support, e.g. residential care, respite and support in the community.

- Improvement in workload management.

However, within conventional occupational therapist-led adult Enablement services, the specialist focus on autism-specific issues such as sensory, social, motor-processing, adaptive interaction is missing. Occupational therapists are utilised to help with sensory integration in Enablement interventions. The ASC Team was seeing individuals on the autistic spectrum who were approaching adulthood and might benefit from being steered towards self-management given the right assessment and the right short-term support provision. Many adult clients exhibit difficulties related to socialisation, communication, sensory processing and behaviours that fall within the remit of occupational therapy.

The ASC Team decided to investigate how it could provide more Enablement-type assistance to its clients. The occupational therapy-trained case manager started to trial some clinical occupational therapy tools (they did not include sensory profiling) and assessing indications of positive outcomes, if any, with clients who worked with an Enablement intervention provided by adult services in a small geographical area. Interventions were carried out by that Enablement service under the guidance of the ASC Team and showed encouraging results.

The specialist Enablement pilot

Based on the results of this trial, in November 2014 Kent County Council agreed to fund a two-year specialist Enablement intervention, which would use an approach for a defined group of individuals with an ASD. The intervention focused on:

- Assessing and providing specialist support for people with autism to address sensory, functional/adaptive and socio-psychological difficulties; addressing, thereby, the core negatively impacting factors of autism and the impact upon the individual; promoting independence; and preventing or reducing the need for long-term packages of support. Support includes helping them make healthy lifestyle choices and informed decisions regarding current and ongoing support strategies; providing options that fit within the individual's broader social context; and actively monitoring and managing issues that impact on their autism.

- Assisting the above within an enabling approach – specifically, to be the first authority to truly test the benefits resulting from an occupational therapist leading a small team of specialist Enablement support workers as they help individuals to self-manage and address limitations posed by autism. This includes not only provision of information, but also assistance in practical application of life skills in the individual context through personalised goal-setting.

Overall, specialist Enablement is based on the two concepts of well-being and self-management. *Well-being* is based on the importance of how each individual thinks and feels about their life. Each individual views their own well-being in relation to their environment and those around them in general. An individual's sense of well-being is clearly subjective but is also affected by how they feel they are viewed by others – positively or negatively. Well-being also covers the sense of pleasure and whether or not an individual feels that their basic human needs are being met (although one's needs and wants are never fully satisfied).

Self-management refers to the support given to individuals to aid and inspire them to become more informed about the issues arising from autism and help them to live their lives in a self-determining way. It is about respecting the choices and individual circumstances of individuals with autism in addressing barriers to self-management and involves goal-setting and problem-solving as key components.

The specialist Enablement service does not mitigate the need for specialist assessment of people with an ASD but aims to contribute to and become an integral part of specialist assessment and support provision in order to assist individuals to attain better outcomes that are personalised and of meaning to them.

The specialist Enablement project started in January 2015, with a further phase of preparatory pilot work involving 13 individuals with an ASD. During this time the team's thoughts about possible research crystallised and we began the planning process involving:

- A literature review, during which the ASC Team found little evidence of similar approaches used for adults with high-functioning autism at the national level.

- Meetings with individuals from Kent County Council's Research Department and the Personal Social Services Research Unit (PSSRU) at the University of Kent at Canterbury to explore what a research project might look like.

- Preparation of written information sheets and consent forms for would-be participants.

- A period of trialling assessment tools and intervention methods, including questionnaires, which involved the ASC Team's professionally trained occupational therapist and two support workers and another two researchers exploring data collection methods.

- Preparing a research proposal and making an application to the Health Research Authority. The ASC Team believes that any evidence collated during the lifespan of the specialist Enablement project could be of national importance in helping UK local authorities to redesign their approaches. Therefore it was decided to register the specialist Enablement project as a research project with the Health Research Authority and the research formally commenced in July 2015.

- Identifying possible participants for the first 12-week research period.

Literature review

Whilst planning the specialist Enablement pilot and designing the research project arising from it, the ASC Team conducted an extensive search of relevant literature related to the support needs of high-functioning adults and people with Asperger syndrome as well as reports on occupational therapy-type interventions being provided. Many of the interventions are focused on social skills, which is an area of significant difficulty for people on the autistic spectrum. According to Harrup (1985, cited in Cappadocia and Weiss 2011), poor social skills are related to concurrent and consequent academic under-achievement, difficulties with peer acceptance and mental health problems. Little evidence could be found of interventions involving occupational-therapy type expertise, with most studies being conducted outside the UK. Much of the support was delivered to children and young people in controlled rather than naturalistic environments and samples were in general very small. Many interventions were delivered in group settings and focused on areas such as social skills/communication, education and employment rather than activities of daily living.

The National Audit Office (2009) looked at support for people with an ASD through adulthood. It found that need between individuals varied and that 'there is scope for better targeted support for people with high-functioning autism/Asperger Syndrome'. It went on to argue that specialised support can improve outcomes for this group in areas such as independent living, improved mental health, increased likelihood of being in employment and better access to services.

Barnard *et al.* (2001) identified that 49 per cent of adults with an ASD live at home with their parents and that many lack independent living skills such as cooking, shopping, managing finances and coping with unstructured time. Beresford *et al.* (2013) looked at transition to adulthood and adult services for young people with ASD who were leaving school or were in early post-school/college years. They conducted interviews with young people as well as carers/families and practitioners and found that 'young people with high-functioning autism and Asperger Syndrome were not eligible for support from transition teams and thus were vulnerable to planning and preparing for leaving school with no ASC-specific input or support' (p. vi). Other findings included that respondents to interviews thought that it was not feasible or appropriate for young people with an ASD to move into independent living in early adulthood; individuals and their families were struggling to know how they could acquire independent living skills; and there was a lack of day and employment activities that were of meaning to individuals. Overall, the research concluded that there was a need for low-intensity intervention delivering preventative support for young people with high-functioning autism and Asperger syndrome.

Westbrook *et al.* (2013) conducted a systematic review to examine the effectiveness of behavioural and social approaches in preparing young people of school age for employment. The review did not include qualitative research. Overall, 85 studies were reviewed but no authoritative findings could be quoted; it was unclear what interventions were effective in producing employment outcomes for people with an ASD. Many interventions used modelling techniques in order to teach vocational skills and behaviours. One study noted 'the importance of age-appropriate, integrated community-based transition-related experiences rather than solely academic instruction in the final years of public education for students with disabilities in order to maximise transition success' (Moon *et al.* 2011, cited in Westbrook *et al.* 2013, p. 35). The review did identify the need for research in this area.

O'Reilly (2014) looked at naturalistic approaches published in peer-reviewed reputable academic journals. Approaches used strategies such as modelling, reinforcement, peer tutoring, social scripts, social problem solving and social skills training groups to teach skills to children with high-functioning autism and Asperger syndrome. The particular strategies explored were chosen because it was thought that they may also benefit different age ranges and contexts. O'Reilly deduced that social problem solving and social skills training might be more appropriate for adolescents and adults.

McCarville Edel Dissertation Abstracts (2014) describes a study involving a very small number of participants (seven) aged 15–24 with high-functioning autism in a peer mentoring intervention. The study investigated if individuals with high-functioning autism would have a greater likelihood of learning independent adaptive daily living skills and improving their social skills following participation in a social group. Data was analysed by visual inspection of graphic displays of each target adaptive daily living skill set in the intervention, withdrawal and reinstatement phases. There was also a monitoring of the effect sizes for each participant. When looking at outcomes, all of the participants demonstrated positive gains, in terms of maintaining and generalising learned skills to the natural home environment. At one-month follow-up, six of the seven participants were reported to be completing, on a weekly basis, at least 50 per cent of the daily living skills they had learned. However, observable gains in behaviour made by participants during the intervention did not readily translate to changes for all contexts, as rated by parents/caregivers. Five out of seven participants did exhibit improved socialisation skills post-intervention.

Palmen and Didden's (2012) study evaluated the effect of a behavioural skills training programme on task engagement in six young adults with high-functioning autism working in a mainstream work-training setting. The training consisted of experimental small-group sessions in a therapy room. Intervention consisted of discrimination training, self-management strategies, behavioural practice, corrective feedback and reinforcement. Data was collected on participants' off-task behaviour and requests for help as well as on the behaviour of staff in the regular setting during regular job tasks (i.e. generalisation). Findings were discussed in relation to future research. When measuring outcomes following intervention, a significant decrease was found in off-task behaviour in the regular setting while performing regular job tasks. No changes were found in requests for help by participants or in the behaviour of staff. Effects were maintained at six-week follow-up. Results need to be treated carefully because the number of participants was low and the different components of the intervention were not closely monitored and investigated; it was thus unclear which element of the intervention was responsible for the results.

The quantitative research conducted by Gantman *et al.* (2011) involved group-based social skills training for 17 young adults with high-functioning autism, aged 18–23. A randomised controlled pilot involved nine young people participating in a treatment programme and eight young people in a control group waiting for treatment. An existing manualised evidence-based adolescent skills training approach (PEERS) was adapted for young adults with high-functioning autism and was delivered over a 14-week period. It was led and monitored by clinical professionals in community settings, with additional input from carers who were expected to provide a certain level of social coaching for participants at home. Data was collected using validated measuring tools, which were administered at start and end of treatment. The results demonstrated significant improvements in social skills as reported by carers. However, the sample in this study was relatively small and part of the intervention included input from individual carers at participants' homes, which meant there was scope for variation in intervention. Furthermore, the behaviour of individual participants within the group may have affected the outcomes; as Gomm, Needham, and Bellman (2000, p. 225) state: 'the results of group intervention trials are particularly problematic for application, since in order to reproduce the research results in practice a practitioner may need to reproduce the group dynamics which developed during the research'.

Bagatell and Mason (2015) carried out a scoping review of US occupational therapy literature from 1980–2013 regarding occupational therapy interventions related to people with ASDs; it involved 115 articles. They found that interventions in that period had increased sevenfold and were primarily focused on children; there were only five studies reporting on interventions for adolescents and there was no reported intervention aimed at adults. Bagatell and Mason note that trends in interventions in the 2010s can be described as 'a more clear commitment to client-centred and occupation-focused outcomes, rather than a focus on behaviour or symptom reduction' (p. 38).

They also note an emerging trend for using family-focus intervention and outcomes. Studies in this period generally highlight the need for support in areas of self-care, education, employment and social activities and participation. The review was somewhat limited in scope because it was restricted to peer-reviewed articles in five occupational therapy journals in the US and thus does not reflect all research in this field. Findings also cannot be generalised because health and care systems are different in other countries.

Haertl *et al.* (2013) published the results of a qualitative, phenomenological study on the lived experience of autism based on interviews and focus groups with adults with high-functioning autism. The majority of the participants received little or no support and only 2 out of 24 individuals accessed occupational therapy services. Interviewees expressed a wish to be part of society but found that difficulties arising from their ASD prevented it, and 'they therefore chose solitary vocational and leisure pursuits' (p. 33). Making friends was challenging and many felt unable to work due to the social demands of a work environment. According to Haertl *et al.*, 'it appeared that structure, support and routine facilitates occupational engagement and motivation for persons with ASD and is an area for potential occupational therapy services' (p. 37).

Gardner, Mulry, and Chalik (2012) reported on a collaborative approach between an entry-level occupational therapy programme and a school-based setting that provided 30 students attending a special needs school for students with language-based and non-verbal disabilities with an opportunity to practise a variety of life skills over a two-day period. The programme aimed at supporting the transition to college and was delivered by occupational therapy Masters students. The interventions took place through social groups and three psychodynamic classes that focused on teaching organisational and life skills and accessing resources and extracurricular activities within the college environment. Relating to outcomes, the study reports positive feedback from parents and the participants themselves regarding the value of mentors in terms of feeling more prepared. The programme led to more formal collaboration between school and college in addressing the transition needs of prospective students. However, the intervention was not based on needs assessment of the individual participants; two days was not considered long enough for allowing generalisation of learnt skills; there was a lack of formal assessment of the efficacy of the intervention, which means that there were no pre-and post-intervention measures to determine its benefits. Instead, feedback was elicited from participants and parents in written form.

Precin *et al.* (2014) reviewed the literature on travel training for young people with ASDs over the period of one year (October 2008–October 2009). They included literature on travel training for young adults with cognitive deficits, arguing that many of those people also had an ASD diagnosis. Various travel training schemes are in existence around the US, generally based within the education system for students with disabilities. In general, the studies showed that community access was often very restricted, most trips taken by participants were accompanied and they went to the same places with the same people. There were no studies that solely assessed occupational therapy involvement. Instead, training was provided by teachers, counsellors and job coaches; there were no tools that measured the benefits of this type of training. A study by Baginski (2008, cited in Precin *et al.* 2014, p. 136) explored the impact of a travel training scheme in Ohio on participants' enhanced perception of independence; travel training was delivered in weekly sessions over an eight-week period and focused on time management, self-organisation, trip planning and self-advocacy skills. When measuring the results, participants were indeed found to have increased their skills in those areas, to feel more confident and to appreciate that being able to travel independently allowed them to spend more time with friends. Precin *et al.* then make the case for occupational therapy involvement in travel training: travel training may be part of an occupational therapist's role within the context of 'enhancing community mobility skills as an instrumental activity of daily living for people with ASDs' (p. 141). What occupational therapists can bring to travel interventions for people with ASDs are money and time management, more awareness about safety, improved communication and social skills, sensory integration and coping strategies, e.g. stress management.

Kandalaft *et al.* (2013) reported on a five-week virtual reality social cognition training programme, aimed at enhancing social skills, social cognition and social functioning. This 10-session pilot programme was provided for 8 adults aged 18–26 with high-functioning autism. The intervention consisted of computer-based simulations which exposed participants in a safe and controlled way to real-life social scenarios, in natural settings, which allowed them to practise managing them. Participants chose avatars to represent themselves, as did the coach (lead clinician) and a guide participant (additional therapist). The participants practised social skills by engaging in interactions using coached techniques and receiving immediate feedback. Performance was measured using validated social cognition measures before and after the intervention and there was a follow-up survey to measure long-term effect. Preliminary findings showed that, overall, the intervention boosted confidence and willingness to try new experiences and increased verbal and non-verbal recognition. Additionally, there were indications that participants demonstrated greater emotional recognition, that is, recognition of others' feelings and tone of voice. Interestingly, there were no increased scores on conversational skills after intervention but participants in the survey thought that this was an area of improvement. The small number of participants and lack of control group limit generalisation but the intervention indicates that further research to validate the preliminary findings is needed.

Research questions

The research project, then, was about providing a specialist Enablement intervention that used a functional, adaptive and sensory approach. The research was aimed at exploring the benefits (or lack thereof) of specialist Enablement for people with high-functioning autism or Asperger syndrome and whether it should be an integral part of support provision for adults on the autistic spectrum. The main question the research wanted to answer was whether the specialist Enablement intervention, using occupational therapy tools and approaches, can facilitate positive change in the individual with high-functioning autism living in the community.

From a local authority perspective, that is, Kent adult social services, the questions to be addressed were:

- Does specialist Enablement prevent the need for high-cost packages of support?

- Is specialist Enablement cost-effective? (Current evidence shows that, while initially Enablement is a more expensive programme compared with a domiciliary service, over a period of time there is a return on investment in both financial terms and the enhanced quality of life experienced by individuals.)

- Do the specialist enabling approaches utilised by occupational therapists increase personal outcome fulfilment/self-management for the client group?

Planning the research

The research team thought long and hard about *selection criteria* and how individuals were to be recruited for both the specialist Enablement intervention and the research. Based on ethical considerations, in order to be provided with specialist Enablement, individuals did *not* have to agree to participate in the research (but in effect all interested individuals put forward for the intervention did agree to become research participants). After much discussion it was agreed that to be eligible for specialist Enablement, individuals must:

- Be aged 18-plus

- Have mental capacity

- Give informed consent

- Have a formal diagnosis of autism without learning disabilities

- Not have presenting needs that impact on ability to participate in the project that require specialist intervention from other services, e.g. severe OCD, untreated ADHD

- Not be subject to safeguarding concerns that prevent the intervention being provided, e.g. where there is evidence, supported by a risk assessment, that the level of violence in an individual's home cannot be satisfactorily addressed to provide specialist Enablement

The ASC Team's research involved all case managers and assessment officers who carried out needs assessments and the specialist Enablement team consisting of an occupational therapist and two assessment officers assisting the occupational therapist. As described in Chapter 4, research participants had either a recent or historic diagnosis of autism and might or might not have had some previous support as a child. The research participants were put forward by practitioners within the ASC Team, who based their decision to refer them for specialist Enablement support upon an occupational therapy priority form as a reference document and the presumption that Enablement will benefit them (as suggested by the needs assessments carried out by practitioners as part of their role). Interested individuals were informed about the intervention and research project verbally and via written information sheets. Those who agreed to participate then gave written consent. It is important to note that, during recruitment, a clear distinction was made between research and practice. Individuals were placed on a waiting list for the specialist Enablement intervention and were recruited in date order. This was necessary because the workers delivering the intervention could work with only a limited number of people at any one time. Where initial assessment identified an urgent need for support, the usual referral process was followed in that individuals were referred to support agencies and such individuals were not put forward for the specialist Enablement and research.

The Kent specialist Enablement process can be summarised as shown in Figure 2.1.

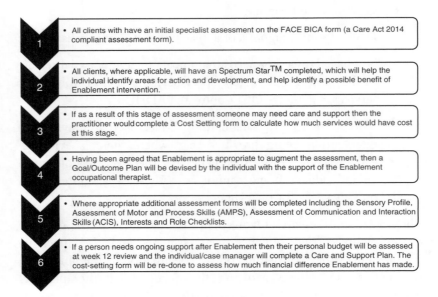

Figure 2.1 The Kent specialist Enablement process

Sample size was determined by how many clients each specialist Enablement worker could engage with over a time-limited period. The researchers were mindful that a certain number of participants was necessary to validate the research results. Robertson and Dearling (2004) suggest that, for statistical analysis, sample size should be no fewer than 30 participants. The researchers recruited an initial 36 individuals to participate in the research.

Regarding *timeframes*, specialist Enablement was to be provided for a 12-week period, with measurements taken at pre-intervention, at the end of intervention (week 12) and, in order to see whether any beneficial effect continued to be experienced, a further 12 weeks after the end of intervention (at week 24).

The intervention was to be conducted in naturalistic *settings*, e.g. research participants' own homes or community settings of their choice and delivered on a 1:1 basis by two support workers under the direction of the trained occupational therapist.

The research was supported by a multi-agency focus group including service users, carers and parents and ASC specialist representatives from health, social care, education and academia. During three meetings over the course of the research year, early successes and challenges were discussed and key themes explored in order to judge whether the approach was delivered in an ethical, person-centred and proportional way. Subjects for consultation included: duration of Enablement, at what age to start, positive behaviour approaches and transferring skills across contexts, to name just a few.

Designing the research methodology

The ASC Team's main priority is to put its clients at the centre of working, which reflects the person-centred ethos in social care. Therefore, the research team wanted to conduct the research in such a way as to give voice to a marginal and marginalised group of people, namely, those with high-functioning autism or Asperger syndrome, so that their knowledge is afforded equal status to the 'scientific' knowledge of the 'experts'. The research was designed to enable participants to select the areas in which *they* wanted to improve their skills and set the goals *they* wanted to achieve. Cresswell (2009) speaks of exploring the meaning an individual ascribes to a social or human problem.

At the time, when considering methodology, the research team first planned to run a randomised controlled trial. Thus a control group who did not participate in the Enablement intervention would also have to be organised. However, when the research proposal was first submitted to the Research Ethics Committee, it was deemed to be inappropriate because the group sizes would be too small to establish and verify the benefits resulting from the intervention; pre- and post-intervention measures were thus suggested. The research design was then changed to a mixed methods approach, with a strong qualitative element that placed the participants' views of and perspectives on desirable social and functional skills at the centre of intervention. The research then followed a time series design, with pre- and post-intervention measurements. This meant using both quantitative assessment tools and qualitative semi-structured interviews to evaluate the impact of the intervention and how it affected (or did not affect) their confidence and self-esteem. Interview scripts were carefully designed bearing in mind Mathers and Huang's reference to poorly designed questionnaires resulting in poor-quality data (cited in Crookes and Davies 2004).

The following tools were used to measure participant skills pre- and post-intervention.

Spectrum Star™

The concept of the star was originally created for use with homeless people and has since been adapted for different client groups. Triangle adapted this concept, named it the Spectrum Star™ (Burns and MacKeith 2012) and licensed it for use with people on the autistic spectrum. The Spectrum Star™ (Figure 2.2) was applied pre- and post-intervention (at 12 and 24 weeks). This tool rates the impact of autism on nine key areas:

- Physical health
- Living skills and self-care
- Well-being and self-esteem
- Sensory differences
- Communication
- Social skills

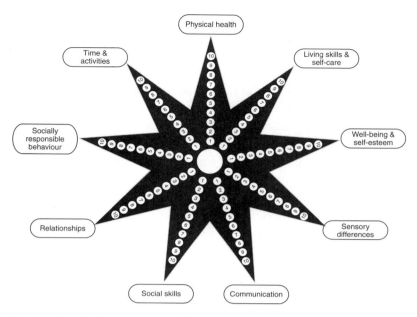

Figure 2.2 Sample client Spectrum Star™
Source: Burns and MacKeith (2012). © Triangle Consulting Social Enterprise Ltd

- Relationships

- Socially responsible behaviour

- Time and activities

The Spectrum Star™ is based on a five-stage journey rating difficulties resulting from autism from 1 (needing most support) to 10 (independent functioning). The findings are then categorised using a simple colour system:

- Red stage – autism is a major barrier

- Orange stage – accepting some support

- Yellow stage – stable

- Light green stage – learning for oneself

- Dark green stage – choice and self-reliance

The Spectrum Star™ was developed by professionals in collaboration with service users and covers the key issues relevant to people on the autistic spectrum. It is a personalised self-assessment and self-evaluation tool which enables service users to identify areas of ability and difficulties and measure progress made. It is a holistic and visual approach to assessment and it is worked on with the service user rather than being imposed on them by professionals; this approach puts the service user at the centre of decision making regarding intervention.

In order to reduce desirability effect, pre- and post-intervention assessments were undertaken by 'neutral' assessors, namely, practitioners within the ASC Team carrying out social care needs assessments who had not been involved in designing or delivering the specialist Enablement intervention. Therefore, in order to use this tool, all practitioners within the ASC Team attended Outcomes Star™ training and licences were obtained from the organisation marketing the tool.

Kent County Council cost-setting tool

This tool is used to set the cost of the number of weekly support hours that have been identified in the needs assessment as required by a client; in the research, it was used as a measure to estimate the cost of support pre-Enablement and then post-Enablement at 12 weeks. The resulting data helps to identify any cost savings made.

Rosenberg Self-Esteem Scale

This was applied before and at the end of the intervention. The tool involves service users responding to 10 statements to ascertain the degree to which an individual feels a sense of self-esteem. Statements are related to feeling good about oneself, having good qualities, feeling no good at all or feeling useless, and the individual rates themself according to the following scale: strongly agree, agree, diasagree or strongly disagree. Scores are set against the responses and the higher the score, the higher is a person's self-esteem.

Semi-structured exit interview

These interviews employed a mixture of closed and open-ended questions to probe service users' perceptions of their experiences and were undertaken at the end of the intervention, at week 12. They were carried out by the chief investigator of the research project and the occupational therapist leading the intervention.

Carers' questionnaire

This questionnaire was developed and validated by Kent County Council for surveys to measure the level of care and support carers provide and any impact on their own lives, e.g. health, time for leisure, employment. This questionnaire was applied, pre-intervention, in person by the case managers and assessment officers who had put the individuals forward for the research. It was re-administered at the end of the intervention either in person or to return by post depending on respondent preference.

Specialist Enablement performance data

This data included assessments, duration of Enablement, hours provided and so on.

The specific occupational therapy tools used during the specialist Enablement intervention are discussed in the next chapter.

Bibliography

Bagatell, N. and Mason, A. (2015) 'Looking backward, thinking forward: Occupational therapy and autism spectrum disorders.' *OTJR: Occupation, Participation and Health* 35, 1, 34–41.

Bancroft, K., Batten, A., Lambert, S., and Madders, T. (2012) *The Way We Are: Autism in 2012*. London: National Autistic Society.

Barnard, J., Harvey, V., Potter, D., and Prior, A. (2001) *Ignored or Ineligible: The Reality for Adults with ASDs*. London: National Autistic Society.

Beresford, B., Moran, N., Sloper, T., Cusworth, L. *et al.* (2013), 'Transition to adult services and adulthood for young people with autistic spectrum conditions.' Accessed on 27/04/2017 at www.york.ac.uk/inst/spru/pubs/pdf/TransASC.pdf.

Burns, S. and MacKeith, J. (2012) *Spectrum Star*™. Triangle Consulting Social Enterprise Ltd. Accessed on 06/08/2017 at www.outcomestar.org.uk.

Cappadocia, M. and Weiss, J. (2011) 'Review of social skills training groups for youth with Asperger syndrome and high functioning autism.' *Research in Autism Spectrum Disorders* 5, 70–78.

Cresswell, J. (2009) *Research Design*. London: Sage.

Crookes, P. and Davies, S. (eds) (2004) *Research into Practice*. London: Bailliere Tindall.

Department of Health (2009) *Autism Act 2009*. London: HMSO.

Department of Health (2010) *Fulfilling and Rewarding Lives: The Strategy for Adults with Autism in England.* London: HMSO.

Department of Health (2014a) *'Think Autism': An Update to the Government Adult Autism Strategy.* London: HMSO.

Department of Health (2014b) *Care Act 2014.* London: HMSO.

Gantman, A., Kapp, S., Orenski, K., and Laugeson, E. (2011) 'Social skills training for young adults with high-functioning autism spectrum disorders: A randomised controlled pilot study.' *Journal of Autism and Developmental Disorders* 42, 1094–1103.

Gardner, J., Mulry, C., and Chalik, S. (2012) 'Considering college? Adolescents with autism and learning disorders participate in an on-campus service-learning program.' *Occupational Therapy in Health Care* 26, 4, 257–269.

Gomm, R., Needham, G., and Bellman, A. (eds) (2000) *Evaluating Research in Health and Social Care.* London: Sage.

Haertl, K., Callahan, D., Markovics, J., and Strouf Sheppard, S. (2013) 'Perspectives of adults living with autism spectrum disorder: Psychosocial and occupational implications.' *Occupational Therapy in Mental Health* 29, 1, 27–41.

Kandalaft, M., Didebani, N., Krawczyk, D., Allen, T. *et al.* (2013) 'Virtual reality social cognition training for young adults with high-functioning autism.' *Journal of Autism and Developmental Disorders* 43, 34–44.

Kent County Council (2005) 'Autism policy framework.' Accessed on 06/08/2017 at https://www.kent.gov.uk/__data/assets/pdf_file/0017/12833/autism-spectrum-disorder-report.pdf.

Kent County Council (2009) 'Autistic Spectrum Disorder Select Committee Report.' Accessed on 06/08/2017 at https://democracy.kent.gov.uk/documents/s14884/ASD%20Report%20FINAL.doc.pdf.

McCarville, E. (2014) 'Peer mentoring intervention teaching adaptive skills to individuals with high functioning autism spectrum disorders.' Unpublished doctoral dissertation, Hofstra University, New York.

National Audit Office (2009) *Supporting People with Autism through Adulthood.* London: Stationary Office.

National Autistic Society (n.d.). 'What is autism?' Accessed on 02/09/2016 at www.autism.org.uk/about/what-is/asd.aspx.

National Institute for Clinical Excellence (2012) 'Autism: Recognition, referral, diagnosis and management of adults on the autistic spectrum.' NICE guidelines (CG142). Accessed on 05/08/2017 at https://grand.tghn.org/site_media/media/medialibrary/2015/03/ASD_NICE_3_.pdf.

O'Reilly, F. (2014) 'Naturalistic approaches to social skills training and development.' In J. K. Luiselli (ed.) *Children and Youth with Autism Spectrum Disorder (ASD): Recent Advances and Innovations in Assessment, Education, and Intervention* (pp. 90–100). Oxford: Oxford University Press.

Palmen, A. and Didden, R. (2012) 'Task engagement in young adults with high-functioning autism spectrum disorders: Generalization effects of behavioral skills training.' *Research in Autism Spectrum Disorders* 6, 4, 1377–1388.

Precin, P., Otto, M., Popalzai, K., and Samuel, M. (2014) 'The role of occupational therapists in community mobility training for people with autism spectrum disorders.' *Occupational Therapy in Mental Health* 28, 2, 129–146.

Roberts, H., Baines, S., Glover, G., and Hatton, C. (2011) *Autism Self-assessment: Issues from Local Authorities.* London: Department of Health.

Robertson, D. and Dearling, A. (2004) *The Practical Guide to Social Welfare Research*. Lyme Regis: Russell House Publishing Ltd.

Rosenberg, M. (1965) *Society and the Adolescent Self-image*. Princeton, NJ: Princeton University Press.

Rosenblatt, M. (2008) *I Exist: The Message from Adults with Autism in England*. London: National Autistic Society.

Valios, N. (2011) 'Why a specialist Asperger's team is the way forward for one council.' *Community Care*, 10 November. Accessed on 27/04/2017 at www.communitycare.co.uk/2011/11/10/why-a-specialist-aspergers-team-is-the-way-forward-for-one-council.

Westbrook, J., Fong, C., Nye, C., Williams, A. *et al.* (2013) 'Pre-graduation transition services for improving employment outcomes among persons with ASDS: A systematic review.' Campbell Collaboration. Accessed on 27/04/2017 at www.campbellcollaboration.org/library/employment-outcomes-persons-with-autism.html.

Chapter 3

An Occupational Therapy-Led Enablement Intervention

Sandra Gasson

This chapter seeks to validate the role of occupational therapy in the planning and delivery of Enablement services for autistic people. It provides lived examples of how the core differences in autism can impact on an autistic person's life. It discusses how occupational therapy principles and approaches can play a significant role in engaging an autistic person to participate in meaningful activities and enable them to experience greater levels of independence; this in turn may then contribute to improving an autistic person's health and well-being. It explains why sensory needs should be addressed as the foundation to higher-level skills and why an Enablement foundation is necessary. It discusses equipment and materials that have been trialled with effect alongside occupational therapy assessments and tools that have supported the identification of personal and environmental factors that can influence an autistic person's ability to engage, and provides case examples of their application.

Role of occupational therapy

In 2010 the Social Care Institute for Excellence recommended occupational therapy involvement in the planning and delivery of Enablement in order to achieve optimum outcomes for service users. Enablement is the process of creating opportunities for people to participate in life's tasks and occupations irrespective of physical or mental impairment or environmental challenges (Christiansen and Townsend 2004). *Occupations* refers to the everyday activities that people do as individuals, in families and with communities to occupy time and bring meaning and purpose to life. Occupations include things people need to, want to and are expected to do (World Federation of Occupational Therapists (WFOT) 2016). Hence, Enablement and occupation are intrinsically linked to promoting people's independence by supporting them to remove environmental barriers and regain or restore practical skills and confidence (Rabiee and Glendinning 2011). Due to its aim of restoring or regaining function, Enablement requires enhanced competencies in assessment and goal setting (Social Services Improvement Agency 2011). Occupational therapists are trained in such skills, have knowledge of the medical, physical, emotional and cognitive impact of disability and are able to ensure that Enablement interventions are tailored to an individual's needs and potential for independence. These abilities and knowledge embody the philosophy and practice of occupational therapy (College of Occupational Therapists 2010a).

Autism is a lifelong developmental disability that affects how people perceive the world and interact with others. As a result, many autistic people see, hear and feel the world differently to other people. Autism is for life as it is not an illness or a disease and it cannot be 'cured'; it affects brain functions, specifically those areas that control social behaviours and communication skills (National Autistic Society 2017a).

While there are approximately 700,000 people in the UK living with autism, which equates to more than 1 in 100 (National Health Service Information Centre 2012), and they all share certain difficulties, being autistic will nevertheless affect them in different ways. Some individuals also have learning disabilities, mental health problems or other conditions, which means they need different levels of support. Some adults with autism do not have an accompanying learning disability or mental health problems, yet services are often provided by learning disability and mental health teams. This has meant that adults with autism, particularly those with *high-functioning autism* such as Asperger syndrome, have not received any services, or have received inappropriate services, where they have been grouped with people with learning disabilities (Abell and Hare 2005), which suggests their needs are being overlooked or ignored by services as a result of their condition being misunderstood (Department of Health 2009b).

Historically, there has been limited information around the long-term outcomes for autistic adults with higher cognitive and language skills. Howlin *et al.* (2004) completed a comprehensive systematic outcome study with this client group and found that the majority (58 per cent) of participants were rated as having 'poor' (requiring specialist residential provision and high levels of support, having no friends outside of their home environment) or 'very poor' (needing high-level hospital care, having no friends and no autonomy) outcomes. A follow-up study by Mawhood, Howlin, and Rutter (2000) of 19 men with autism found that, although the majority improved with time, all participants continued to have difficulties with communication, social relationships and independence. Billstedt, Gillberg, and Gillberg (2005) found, in their follow-up study of 120 participants who had been diagnosed with ASD as children and followed through their adolescence and adulthood, that they had even poorer outcomes that were related to medical problems, deterioration during adolescence, such as exhibiting self-injurious and violent behaviours, and lack of independent living and employment. This highlights that, regardless of where someone sits on the autistic spectrum, they can continue to have difficulties into adulthood; their need for support and their probable outcomes are determined not only by their abilities and the challenges they face but also, in many cases, by their access to services and the quality of such services (Koenig and Kinnealey 2010).

While adults with autism vary enormously from each other they all share the two core features of autism: difficulties with social communication and social interaction. Some individuals have little interest in interacting with others, while some are keen to socialise and form relationships. However, many autistic adults are confused by the 'unwritten rules' of social interaction and inadvertently make mistakes and, as a result, find interacting with others a stressful experience.

Other difficulties as previously described in Chapter 1 can include restricted, repetitive patterns of behaviour, interests or activities. For example, individuals may develop an overwhelming interest in something, follow inflexible routines or rituals, make repetitive body movements and have sensory needs – or indeed a combination of all of these.

Our observations and experience of working with such individuals have informed us that many clients can present with high levels of anxiety and frequently report that this situation is made worse by the stress of living in a 'neurotypical' world. While some autistic adults have been able to put coping strategies in place, many still struggle and ask for support to address their difficulties. They can present as being socially awkward or display inappropriate behaviours, and need support to gain a greater awareness of these difficulties, particularly when they encounter rejection when trying to make friends, develop relationships or find work. It is important to acknowledge here that, while many individuals with autism can experience challenges with activities of daily living, not all autistic individuals think autism is a problem. These people need to be accepted and accommodated as individuals in their own right; they do not need to be 'cured' or trained in how to 'pretend' to be neurotypical (Beardon and Edmonds 2007). However, every culture has social norms that need to be acknowledged to a degree, and some autistic adults do need support and greater insight to understand how their behaviours may not adhere to the accepted norm. Vermeulen (2012, p. 151) asserts that, 'It is not about knowing if a certain behaviour is appropriate, but about knowing when a behaviour is appropriate or not.'

Vermeulen goes on to discuss the significance of context in relation to behaviour; that is, what is completely acceptable behaviour in one context may be unacceptable in another, and vice versa. Context determines the appropriateness of people's behaviour, and those who are blind to context have difficulty guessing if a certain behaviour is socially acceptable or not. This is the case for people with autism and we have encountered numerous examples of our clients misinterpreting social situations; for example:

> *Paul is a 43-year-old autistic man who is highly anxious and seeking to find paid work. He often talks about topics when it is not appropriate and his overall presentation, in particular his personal care, is poor. He has been called to interview on numerous occasions but has still not managed to secure a job. Paul has little to no awareness that he needs to be clean and presentable or that his chances in interviews are affected by this issue. He is simply not aware of what is expected, of the social rules inherent in this situation.*

Another difficulty often experienced by autistic adults is their lack of awareness of non-verbal communication – in other words, they are unable to read other people's body language, facial expressions and tone of voice and, as a consequence, often do not understand intuitively the emotions another person is communicating, which can result in their failing to pick up on the social cues.

Janice is a 27-year-old autistic woman who lives alone and enjoys travelling on the bus to pass the time. She is keen to form relationships and wants a boyfriend. She often speaks to strangers and talks at length about her chosen interest with no awareness that listeners are presenting closed body language or trying to make excuses to leave the conversation. Janice can find it difficult to understand the perspectives of others and may pitch into people's conversations talking about her own interests without noticing that they are unfamiliar with that topic and struggling to follow her conversation. This often leads to misunderstandings and Janice placing herself at risk.

Use of language in communication can be another issue for autistic adults because they find it difficult to recognise how words are applied in everyday situations, which can be very confusing.

Ben is 23 years old. He has an excellent vocabulary but is not aware of how to adapt it to different situations. For example, when purchasing items at the supermarket he told the cashier he was looking for a girlfriend and asked her if she was married.

Additional communication difficulties include turn taking, changing the topic of conversation, giving responses and maintaining coherence throughout a conversation, alongside difficulties recognising and expressing their own emotions.

William is 22 years old and, as a keen photographer, used to attend a local photography group with his father. William's photographs attracted much attention and he was initially approached by other members of the group. William would talk excessively about his chosen interest and not give any thought to others who were trying to enter the conversation. If someone else tried to express their own views, William would simply carry on talking about his subject. He was often pre-occupied with his own agenda and would miss opportunities to take turns in an appropriate manner. William did not understand why people avoided him when he turned up for group meetings and made their excuses when he tried to talk to them. William decided to leave the group. He became very depressed and withdrawn, not wanting to leave his bedroom or interact with his family. His mother reported that he had been prescribed medication and referred to his local mental health service.

Underpinning occupational therapy is the belief that occupation and activity are fundamental to a person's health and well-being within the context of their various environments. Alongside a person's ability to carry out activities are roles that they need, want and are expected to fulfil in their daily life, and together these are seen as their occupational performance. Occupational therapists understand how a person's health and well-being can affect their occupational performance and participation. Therefore, this may serve to justify why occupational therapists have a key role in enabling autistic adults to achieve their chosen goals through modification of their desired or required occupations, by supporting them to learn new skills and approaches and to adapt their environments (or a combination of them); occupational therapists see activity in itself as an effective medium for remediation or an agent of change (College of Occupational Therapists 2017).

Occupational therapy focuses on enhancing participation in the performance of activities of daily living. Activities of daily living are vital to the independence of individuals with autism and considered essential to adulthood. Daily activities such as bathing, cleaning teeth, preparing and cooking a meal, carrying out domestic chores, using public transport, crossing the road, shopping and budgeting can be problematic, and are found to be a particular area of difficulty for those with higher cognitive abilities (Duncan and Bishop 2013).

This supports our own observations that many autistic adults are still heavily reliant on others such as parents and carers for many of their activities of daily living. Bancroft *et al.* (2012) concur, stating that 70 per cent of autistic adults report that they are not getting the help they need from social services and that, with more support, they would feel less isolated. A carer is someone who provides (or intends to provide), paid or unpaid, a substantial amount of care on a regular basis for someone of any age who is unwell or, for whatever reason, cannot care for themselves independently (adapted from the Carers Act 1995). Occupational therapists have a key role in utilising the strengths of the autistic adult, the environment and the community in which they live and function. They can work with the autistic adult, their families and/or carers and their communities where appropriate, to identify solutions and enhance their ability to engage in the occupations they want, need or are expected to do (College of Occupational Therapists 2017).

Many families report that they have received inadequate (or no) specialist support over the years. This, coupled with the fact that their autistic son or daughter finds social interaction difficult and has had limited opportunities to engage in socialising with others or to access working environments in which people understand them, has subsequently left family members worrying about the future when they are no longer able to care for the autistic individual. This situation can become a growing burden for aging parents (Graetz 2010) and the cause of increasing levels of stress (Abbeduto *et al.* 2004; Bouma and Schweitzer 1990; Dumas *et al.* 1991; Montes and Halterman 2007; Seltzer *et al.* 2010).

The occupational therapy intervention process

The occupational therapy intervention process is based on assessment. Assessment is defined by the European Network of Occupational Therapy in Higher Education (ENOTHE 2004) as a process of collecting and interpreting information about the person and their environment, using observation, testing and outcome measurement, in order to inform decision making and monitor change.

The results of evaluations are personalised to reflect a variety of strategies and techniques to help autistic adults to maximise their ability to engage in meaningful daily activities whether these are occurring at home, college, work and/or in the community. Individual progress is measured in terms of improved performance, enhanced participation in meaningful activities, personal satisfaction, improved health and well-being and successful transitions to new situations or roles (American Occupational Therapy Association 2010).

Occupational therapy can support autistic adults to modify tasks and their environments to balance their needs and abilities. This includes the identification of the skills they need to accomplish a task, practising those tasks whilst minimising external distractions, utilising visual materials to aid independence and learning, trialling equipment to ease anxiety and utilising mobile technology and apps. Occupational therapists can devise strategies to help the individual to transition from one setting to another, from one person to another and from one life phase to another. Occupational therapy approaches, knowledge and skills can thus offer great value to the wider social care assessment and, moreover, enable and enhance the lives of autistic adults.

Outcome measurement can demonstrate the effectiveness of interventions for autistic adults and support occupational therapists in guiding their decision making and/or intervention. In addition, they can use outcome measures, especially standardised measures, to add to the body of evidence supporting the role of occupational therapists (College of Occupational Therapists 2015) and, what's more, support much-needed research in the area of autism.

The specialist Enablement intervention

Riley (2012) suggests that, when occupational therapists are included in Enablement services, they contribute to the delivery of cost-effective services by reducing expenditure on home and residential care. Glendinning *et al.* (2010) support this view and also suggest that the Enablement intervention has significant potential to reduce ongoing care and support costs despite its higher upfront costs compared with traditional home care. Through emerging evidence in this area it is clear that not only can occupational therapists engage in Enablement provision but they are also best placed to support the delivery of such a service; what is more, they can enhance the lives of those living with ASCs (Nicholson and Kerslake 2011).

To truly enhance the lives of those living with an ASC, occupational therapists need assessment tools that reflect their unique focus and gather information about a person's everyday life and their reasons for doing what they do (Law 2005). Adults with autism vary greatly in their individual learning styles, their problem areas and their response to intervention. Since adults with a diagnosis of autism present a somewhat unique clinical picture, innovative approaches to intervention are required based upon an occupational therapy frame of reference (the term 'frame of reference' describes using specific knowledge to provide an approach to practice; Duncan 2006, p. 338). Other factors also need to be considered, such as the occupational therapy goals the autistic person has agreed to and the duration of the Enablement intervention because this will affect choice of intervention; some frames of reference require long-term interventions to allow for the sequential development of skills (Bloomer and Rose 1989).

Many people on the autistic spectrum experience high levels of anxiety and although they vary enormously from each other they all share difficulties with social communication and social interaction. They may find it hard to hold a conversation, understand other people, think flexibly or plan ahead. What is more, they may have sensory processing differences such as aversions to loud noises, bright lights, being touched and strong smells. All of these difficulties can impact on their ability to maintain/sustain their focus in everyday tasks. They may have other co-morbidities such as ADHD; mental health problems such as depression, anxiety and compulsions; and physical difficulties, motor problems or functional difficulties such as problems with sleep. All need equal consideration. For these reasons, effective and timely planning is essential and serves to justify why autistic people need realistic timeframes that not only reflect their complex needs but also their ability to learn new skills to enhance their independence. Feedback from individuals who have engaged with the Enablement intervention confirms that 12 weeks is often just a start; many report that they would have liked longer. When intervention time is limited, Fisher (2009) suggests that the following frames of reference be utilised:

- *Acquisitional* – reacquiring or developing occupational skills

- *Compensatory* – adapting occupation to compensate for decreased occupational skills

- *Educational* – providing occupation-based educational programmes focused on performance of activities of daily living

Person-centred goals and outcome measures

Occupational therapy can focus on person-centred goals, quality of life and needs of the wider family. Carers must be told about their rights to a carer's assessment under the Care Act 2014 because support services may well be offered.

The occupational therapy process is designed to gain an understanding of the individual's skills, strengths and limitations while engaging in meaningful activities of daily living, and focuses on finding ways to enable individuals to explore new levels of independence (Mickel 2010).

Additionally, occupational therapy can reliably measure improvements and outcomes. As previously stated, our social care team has found the

Spectrum Star™ (Burns and MacKeith 2012) to be of great benefit because this person-centred evidence-based tool for supporting and measuring change looks at the life of the autistic person from their perspective. It helps us to build rapport initially and then later serves as part of initial assessment and a baseline for occupational therapy upon which to work out and agree on realistic person-centred goals. Person-centred planning can present challenges for the autistic person, since many people with autism experience difficulties with communication, abstract thinking and expressing their aspirations – all of which are at the core of this process. It is thus vital that autistic people are given access to those who understand the condition. This may be an appropriate point to mention the importance of working closely with the autistic person's family to help ascertain what the person wants to achieve in life. Many autistic individuals struggle with abstract concepts; aspirations, dreams and desires can thus be difficult for them to imagine or visualise as they find it difficult to picture a life other than the one they are currently living. For some autistic people, thinking about their future in unclear terms may also cause anxiety (National Autistic Society 2007); for example:

> *Dillon aspires to be a pilot while Nigel wants to be a bus driver. Both have limited understanding about how realistic these occupational goals are or how to achieve them.*

Person-centred planning is a key concept for the whole team, and in particular the occupational therapist, because enabling a client to set and work towards their own goals, achieving small incremental steps, helps them develop their self-confidence and self-esteem sooner than a sense of failure (ibid).

An asset-based approach is also used for every person. Hudson (2010) defines an 'asset' as any factor or resource which enhances the ability of individuals, communities and populations to maintain and sustain health and well-being. These assets can operate at the level of the person, family or community as protective and promoting factors to buffer against life's stresses. This approach utilises and builds upon the abilities, skills, knowledge and other resources of people, families, groups and communities with the objective of promoting and strengthening the factors that support good health and well-being, enabling those individuals to gain more control over their lives and personal circumstances.

Occupational therapy tools and assessments

This section discusses some of the assessment tools used by the occupational therapist during the specialist Enablement intervention. We then consider sensory processing, which is a fundamental element of the intervention and links to one of our main tools – Brown and Dunn's (2002) Adolescent/Adult Sensory Profile™.

Most of the assessments and tools we use have been selected based on Kielhofner's (2008) Model of Human Occupation (MOHO). MOHO is a theory that explains aspects of human behaviour addressed in occupational therapy practice and provides tools to apply that theory to practice. MOHO conceptualises humans as comprising of three interrelated components: volition, habituation and performance capacity. Volition refers to the motivation for occupation, habituation refers to the process by which occupation is organised into routines, and performance capacity refers to the physical and social environments in which it takes place. Thus, MOHO aims to understand occupation and problems of occupation that occur in terms of its primary concepts plus environmental factors. MOHO can be used with anybody who is experiencing difficulties with their occupational life and is designed to be used across the life span (Kielhofner and Neville 1983). MOHO assessments provide a structured and comprehensive assessment by systematically identifying the personal and environmental factors influencing a person's occupational adaptation and providing a person-centred measurement that has been used to suit different situations and also tested to ensure reliability and clinical utility (Kramer, Kielhofner, and Forsyth 2007).

Assessment of Motor and Process Skills

The Assessment of Motor and Process Skills (AMPS; Fisher and Jones 2010) is an observational evaluation designed to be used by occupational therapists. Users must attend a specialised training course in the standardised AMPS administration procedures and a five-day course on rater calibration. Potential AMPS raters must complete 10 live observations following the course and submit this data for rater calibration. Rater calibration allows each rater's severity and scoring reliability to be determined. The AMPS is designed to evaluate the quality of an individual's performance of activities of daily living in natural, task-relevant environments. The occupational therapist will work with the individual to identify their strengths and limitations and support them to identify which activities are problematic and which are a priority for them. Once this is established, and if the tasks identified are activities of daily living (ADL), the occupational therapist may choose to administer the AMPS as a standardised performance analysis of ADL task performance.

The AMPS is used to score the quality of 16 ADL motor and 20 ADL process performance skills. Each occupational performance skill is scored according to how much clumsiness or physical effort, time and space inefficiency (i.e. organisation of time and space), safety risk and/or need for assistance the person demonstrates when enacting these ADL task actions. For example, if a man is observed while he is preparing his breakfast of a glass of milk and a bowl of cereal, he is scored based on how effectively he reaches for, grasps and lifts the carton of milk from the refrigerator and then transports it to the counter. He is given lowered scores on relevant ADL motor items if he demonstrates observable clumsiness or increased physical effort, safety risk, and/or need for assistance when carrying out each respective ADL task action. Similarly, he is scored based on whether or not he searches for and locates the milk carton in the refrigerator, chooses the carton of milk (and not the carton of orange juice), takes the carton of milk to the same location as the glass, and initiates performing each ADL task action without any observable pauses. The occupational therapist can then interpret the results to facilitate occupation-based intervention planning. The benefits of using the AMPS with autistic individuals are that they can choose ADL tasks that are meaningful, relevant, present a challenge and are the desired focus of occupational therapy intervention. It can also provide the occupational therapist with a powerful and sensitive tool that can assist with planning their intervention and, what's more, document any change. The AMPS demonstrates the efficacy of the occupational therapy intervention in a cost-effective and client-centred way. The assessment does not require any special equipment and can be administered in the individual's home within a 40-minute period. However, some of the limitations of AMPS include the requirement for the occupational therapist to attend AMPS training and calibration courses and the fact that it would not be considered for autistic individuals who have no need to develop or who are unwilling to participate in simple daily life tasks.

Case example: Rodney

Rodney is 22 years old and an only child. He received an ASC diagnosis at the age of four. Both of his parents have died and he has moved from what was the family home to live in his own flat for the first time. He is 5 feet 10 inches tall and obese. He has been referred for Enablement as his case manager is concerned that he was increasingly becoming unable to manage living independently. He has been living in his flat for a year but has not attempted to organise or maintain his home environment. He has been eating pre-prepared convenience foods, purchased from his local shop – a diet that contributes to his obesity. He has little awareness of the value of his money, which has accumulated from his benefits. He reports feeling isolated and being exploited by someone who has come to the door asking for money. Rodney has poor personal hygiene and is growing more anxious about his situation. Rodney is able to identify his difficulties carrying out many household tasks, stating that his parents used to do these and that he did not have to worry about them. Rodney reports that he does not know how to cook meals or clean his flat and that he is unsure whether he will ever be able to do such tasks. Because Rodney is having difficulty performing activities of daily living, the occupational therapist chooses to use the AMPS to gather information on his motor and process skills as the assessment will also highlight Rodney's strengths and limitations in performing the ADL necessary for community living that he wants to improve. From the standardised tasks available in the AMPS, Rodney is able to choose two that are appropriately challenging. He chooses to prepare a cheese sandwich and hand wash the dishes as he considers these activities to be meaningful in his life. The occupational therapist then administers the formal AMPS. Rodney scores 2.0 on the motor scale and 1.1 on the process scale. Both scores indicate that he is on the borderline where skill deficits begin to negatively impact on ADL performance and where the majority of individuals experience difficulty with independent living. Rodney demonstrates ineffective motor skills throughout his performance, that is, in the following areas:

- *Body position*
  - *Positioning and bending his body appropriate to the task*
- *Obtaining and holding objects*
  - *Co-ordinating two body parts to stabilise task objects*
  - *Gripping to maintain a secure grasp on task objects*

Rodney's process skills demonstrate further difficulties in:

- *Sustaining performance*
  - ○ *Heeds — the purpose of his task*
- *Applying knowledge*
  - ○ *Chooses — the appropriate tools and materials for the task*
  - ○ *Inquires — about the necessary information*
- *Temporal organisation*
  - ○ *Initiates — actions or steps without hesitation*
- *Organising space and objects*
  - ○ *Organises — tools and materials in a logical, orderly and spatially appropriate way*
  - ○ *Navigates — hands and body appropriately around objects*
  - ○ *Restores — putting away his tools and materials, cleaning work surfaces*
- *Adapting performance*
  - ○ *Notices/responds — to non○ verbal task○ related environmental cues*
  - ○ *Accommodates — actions to overcome problems*
  - ○ *Benefits — from the experience to prevent recurring problems*

INTERPRETATION OF RODNEY'S RESULTS In the area of motor skills, the following observations were made during his AMPS assessment. Because he positioned himself too close to the fridge, he constantly banged the fridge door into himself. He struggled to bend down to access task-related objects from a low cupboard. These problems were exacerbated by the fact that his kitchen area was small, his physique made his body movements in relation to the fridge more difficult and he used a cupboard close to the floor to store essential everyday items. Rodney had difficulty gripping objects, which, later transpired, arose from a lack of practice in using his fine motor skills. Throughout his life he had relied on gross motor skills and failed to develop skills with his hands and fingers thus limiting his performance on the AMPS tasks.

In the area of process skills, Rodney had difficulty preparing his cheese sandwich. He did not incorporate some of the ingredients he had agreed to include and, when asked why, stated that he had 'forgotten' to do so, thus illustrating why he found it difficult to complete all of the steps involved in making the sandwich. The same difficulty was seen in other skill areas, such as 'restores' – he did not return items to their original location after he finished his task. Rodney also appeared to misunderstand some of the information that he was given prior to the task, a situation made more difficult when he did not seek clarification. Rodney hesitated throughout the task and organised his workspace so that it was cluttered. When cutting the sandwich, he used the knife in such a manner that he could have injured himself. He demonstrated difficulties adapting to his environment and responding appropriately to environmental changes.

In spite of Rodney's difficulties in terms of both motor and process skills, he was competent in many areas. His strengths suggested that he did not require assistance at any time during the observation and that he would benefit from specific support to help him engage safely in activities of daily living. Specific recommendations to manage Rodney's limitations were to adapt his kitchen to accommodate his motor needs, such as moving the fridge to the other side of the kitchen to accommodate his unusually large stature; positioning the fridge so that he could open the door fully to access its contents; and fitting a cupboard for essential everyday items at eye level to avoid the necessity of bending. His process scale difficulties highlighted the need for regular assistance with some tasks and prompting for others, as well as the need for support when problem solving in difficult situations.

The Enablement support provided Rodney with pictorial recipes and shopping lists; technology (telecare) whereby a bogus call button was installed (a panic button that generates a silent alarm call to the telecare team providing round the clock monitoring) – this was deemed appropriate as Rodney agreed that he needed reassurance when answering the front door to unexpected visitors as he had been financially exploited by rogue callers; and daily prompts to help him remember to take his medication. Rodney was also shown how to set the alarm on his mobile phone so that he could use it to remember appointments. Rodney also started to attend a community group and was referred to an in-house service to help individuals find work. Rodney continued to do well with minimal support (two hours per week), and following his Enablement period gained a new awareness of his own capabilities, which significantly increased his sense of self-worth and contributed to him securing a part-time job in a local store over the Christmas period. The AMPS provided critical objective information relating to Rodney's occupational performance and helped the occupational therapist to make decisions about his intervention. The AMPS was also useful in terms of documenting the need for Rodney to have an ongoing support package that would further enhance his skills and continue to enable him to function safely in the community.

Assessment of Communication and Interaction Skills

Social interaction has long been recognised as an important factor in people's daily lives. We are continuously encountering and interacting with others (Hamilton, Sherman, and Lickel 2005). Individuals with an ASC often find it hard to communicate effectively and so can struggle to form and sustain meaningful relationships with others. Much empirical evidence suggests that interpersonal relationships are linked to self-reported happiness (Bruni 2010), which suggests that people with an ASC could be at greater risk of declining mental health if they are not able to interact effectively with others. Galanopoulos (2014) concurs, reporting that mental illness can be more common in people with an ASC than in the general population and, unfortunately, that the mental health of people on the spectrum is often overlooked. Occupational therapists have a key role to play in enabling activity and social interaction (Krupa, Woodside, and Pocock 2010). Social skills training may help here, and a great deal of evidence supports its effectiveness with people experiencing mental illness (Dilk and Bond 1996; Greenblatt, Becerra, and Serafetinides 1982; Kopelowicz, Liberman, and Zarate 2006). Occupational therapists can draw on assessments such as the Assessment of Communication and Interaction Skills (ACIS; Forsyth *et al.* 1998). This useful observational assessment is designed to gather data on the skills that an individual demonstrates when communicating and interacting with others in an occupational or group setting.

This assessment is composed of behaviours or action 'verbs' that represent an individual's performance skills. It covers three domains of communication and interaction: physicality, information exchange and relations. Each skill is rated on a four-point scale (4 = competent, 3 = questionable, 2 = ineffective, 1 = deficit). The occupational therapist uses ACIS to rate an individual on each of the communication and interaction performance skills after observing that individual engaging in a relevant social context.

The ACIS notes whether a particular skill is present and how this affects the ongoing social action but will not identify underlying causes of an observed lack of communication and interaction skills. For example, the ACIS verb 'articulates' orients the observer to ask whether the person being observed produces speech that can be understood and readily heard by others and how this affects ongoing social action. Should an articulation problem be noted, the occupational therapist can then go on to discover its possible sources; it may be due to the individual's motor problems, their accent or the fact that they mumble words when they are anxious.

The ACIS is not commonly used with people higher-functioning on the spectrum. However, because their difficulties are generally similar to those of lower-functioning individuals, we have found it useful for exploring the domains described below:

> *Physicality* – In the process of interacting with other physical beings we may touch, approach or leave them. Whether we choose to stand near to, face or look at them, how we arrange and move our bodies and the facial expressions we make have important effects on how others perceive us and understand what we mean or intend. These physical behaviours, whether intentional or unintentional, can affect how well we are able to work or socialise with others. To sum up, we actively use our physical selves in relation to others and *how* we do so greatly affects our success or failure when interacting with others.

> *Information exchange* – Competent exchange of information is a skill that is important to occupational behaviour. To give and receive such information, we have to produce sounds that can be heard or signs that can be seen, recognised and interpreted. We must be able to express coherent ideas and thoughts, to connect what we are saying with what others are saying and

doing and to acquire and give information relevant to the tasks we are performing.

Relations – As social beings we can feel a bond of connection to others or alienation from them alongside being able to readily react emotionally to how we think others perceive us, treat us and care about us. We expect certain behaviours of people and find other behaviours offensive or unacceptable. Subsequently, to be able to carry out effective occupations that involve others, we must be able to engage in behaviours that facilitate how others feel about us and the task in hand. These include being able to recognise and comply with normative behaviour, follow what is expected given our roles and recognise and produce appropriate behaviour for the task, which additionally means that we need to be able to 'read' others and interpret what they might be thinking and feeling about our actions towards them.

Occupational therapists may wish to evaluate communication and interaction skills for many reasons. High-functioning autistic adults are particularly likely to experience challenges in all three domains, which can adversely affect their ability to engage with others, find and sustain work and engage in social and self-care activities. The ACIS can help the occupational therapist to identify key areas on which to base meaningful intervention goals for individuals with high-functioning autism. Additionally, the ACIS can be a useful assessment tool to analyse people's *risk* when they are out and about in social environments. It can also provide evidence supporting a need for a community support package.

Modified Interest Checklist

The Modified Interest Checklist (Kielhofner 2008) gathers information on a person's patterns of interest and engagement in activities in the past, currently and in the future. The main focus is on leisure interests that influence activity choices (Kielhofner and Naville 1983). The checklist is suitable for adolescents and adults and as such can be used to assist in the selection of topics for discussion or to stimulate discussion where social communication is difficult. It has been found to be a useful initial tool for building rapport and gaining an understanding of an individual's interests. Furthermore, it can be used to help plan meaningful activities for the individual to engage in at home and in the wider community, thus boosting their opportunities to socialise, improving their communication skills and improving their health and well-being. The value of activity should not be underestimated – it fills our days and we all need purposeful tasks to survive and flourish (Wilcock 1993).

Kielhofner (2008) notes that, without activity, time weighs heavily upon us; we are all moved to fill or occupy our time; and that we mark the passing of time by what we have been doing (cooking, working, eating and so on). Thus, what we do fills our present and we anticipate the future according to what we have planned to do. Well-being results from achieving a balance between three types of activity: self-care, leisure and work/productivity (Håkansson, Dahlin, and Sonn 2006). Well-being can be maintained by establishing roles and routines that incorporate activities based on our values and interests; in turn, this helps us to develop relationships and gives us a sense of belonging (Kielhofner 2008). Longitudinal research indicates that, during adolescence, many individuals with an ASC show increased interest in social relationships (Mesibov 1983; Mesibov and Handlan 1997; Volkmar and Kiln 1995), but continue to find the social realm very difficult to negotiate into adulthood (Church, Alinsanski, and Amanullah 2000). The majority repeatedly report finding it difficult to make friends and state that they long for relationships like their peers. Because activities (occupations) describe who we are, they change how we feel about ourselves; thus, what we choose to do changes how we feel and has the power to change our lives. Occupational therapy can explore and facilitate these changes through an individual's interests – a key aspect of engaging with people with an ASC. Establishing a balance of activities in everyday life creates greater opportunities for improved health and well-being (Håkansson et al. 2006). What is more, by using the Interest Checklist occupational therapists can ascertain what is meaningful to an individual and then initiate purposeful activities that reflect their values – meaningfulness is what motivates performance (Trombly 1995).

Role Checklist

The Role Checklist (Oakley *et al.* 1986) was designed to enable occupational therapists to acquire information on an individual's perception of their participation in 10 occupational roles throughout their life. It also assesses the importance that individuals place on such occupational roles. Individuals with an ASC often have diminished roles in key normative areas, including 'work'. The Department of Health (2009a) acknowledges this and suggests that only 15 per cent of adults with autism are in paid employment. The most important question posed by the Role Checklist is: 'How important is the role to you?' This is because some of the occupational roles they list may not be of relevance or interest to the individual with an ASC so they may not necessarily experience or recognise their loss. Through discussion, individuals with an ASC can be helped to express their satisfaction with their performance of the 10 roles. The Role Checklist can also be used together with the Modified Interest Checklist (Kielhofner 2008) to help support discussion, future session planning and monitor outcomes.

Sensory profile

Sensory processing is at the heart of the Kent County Council Enablement intervention. This is because it is widely reported that people with an ASC experience sensory processing differently (Baranek 2002; Crane, Goddard, and Pring 2009) and these differences can be experienced across all senses (Mayes *et al.* 1999). These sensory differences impact on the daily lives of people with autism in various ways (Dunn, Myles, and Orr 2002; Grandin 2006; Grandin and Scariano 1986; Williams 1999), including in relation to skills that support performance, such as engagement and attention, and skills that enable the learning of new motor skills (Cosby 2010; Jasmin 2009).

As Ayres (1979, pp. 4–5), occupational therapist and founder of sensory integration therapy, explains:

> The brain locates, sorts and orders sensations, somewhat like the way a traffic light directs moving cars. When sensations flow in a well-organised or integrated manner, the brain uses those sensations to form perceptions, behaviours and learning. When the flow is disorganised, life can be like a rush-hour traffic jam.

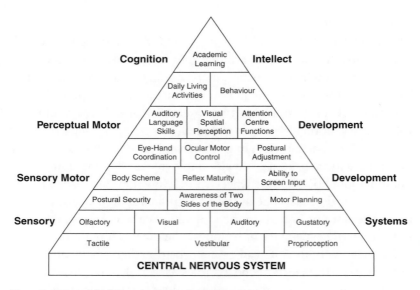

Figure 3.1 Pyramid of Learning © Taylor/Trott 1991

Ayres further believes that sensory integration is integral to the process of healthy development, explaining that 'the brain must organise all of our sensations if a person is to move and learn and behave in a productive manner' (2005, p. 5). In other words, the integration of sensory information from the seven sensory systems facilitates the acquisition of higher-level skills and comprises the foundation of learning. This suggests that sensory processing is vital because it provides a firm foundation for higher-level cognitive and motor skills. Without this firm foundation, autistic people with sensory difficulties have nothing to support higher-level skills and their ability to achieve higher-level cognitive tasks such as activities of daily living is compromised. The pyramid of learning model (see Figure 3.1) is the central focus of our initial Enablement work. We use it as the foundation from which to ascertain the needs of autistic people and on which to build our specialist Enablement framework.

Sensory integration theory supports the delivery of occupational therapy intervention in a number of ways. First, through direct sensory integration treatment; second, through sensory strategies; and, third, through consultation/coaching (College of Occupational Therapists 2013). The College of Occupational Therapists (2010b) recommends that all occupational therapists provide only those services and use those techniques in which they are qualified by education, training and/or experience and are competent to deliver. The Enablement intervention used strategies based on sensory integration theory. These include environmental adaptations and the specific use of equipment such as noise-cancelling headphones for those over-responsive to sound, and weighted blankets and/or hoodies for those seeking proprioceptive input, which can be calming for those who are easily overwhelmed by sensory stimulation. It is recommended that sensory-based interventions be informed by the findings of thorough assessments and individualised according to each person's sensory problems (College of Occupational Therapists 2013). Brown and Dunn's (2002) Adolescent/Adult Sensory Profile™ can contribute to helping autistic adults and their families to understand the nature of their sensory differences and supporting them in self-regulating their responses to stimuli. Furthermore, it can help the occupational therapist to recommend strategies that encourage the autistic person to engage in activities of daily living. Sensory differences can thus play an important part in how autistic people experience their world. It is important to mention here, however, that some autistic people actually find that their sensory differences result in a pleasurable experience. Learning how the senses of each individual autistic person function is one crucial key to understanding them (O'Neill 1999) and any future support they may need.

Heffernan (2016) describes the sensory system as a subconscious part of the nervous system, which is made up of a series of cells and nerves carrying messages around the body. Its job is to take in, process and form outcomes in response to the environment. It is also designed to protect the body from danger and relies on 'pre-programmed' information and past experiences. We have more than the five traditionally recognised senses – that is, more than sight (vision), hearing (audition), taste (gustation), smell (olfaction) and touch (somatosensation). Vision involves more than seeing things; it includes our ability to see, recognise and process the information taken in by our eyes. It deciphers whether things are moving and judges colours. Our ears receive auditory information at various pitches, and how we process sound waves enables us to form meaning from what we hear. Our nose is the receptor for olfactory information, which is also linked to memories and emotions associated with particular scents. Our mouth has many receptors that decipher information from different flavours. Our lesser-known senses are proprioception, which involves receptors in our muscles, joints and tendons. These receptors provide information about the body's position and movements so that we unconsciously understand where our arms and legs are at a given time without having to look. Our vestibular receptors are deep within the ear. These receptors consist of three semi-circular canals filled with fluid. As the fluid moves, our receptors determine the position of our body in space. Gravity pulls on our body, and to remain upright our body is constantly trying to determine its position in space.

People with autism can experience hyper-sensitivity – an over-reaction of the senses – which can change in relation to how an individual is feeling. Often it generates an overwhelming need to get away from a particular stimulus, especially in environments that contain an overwhelming array of sensory inputs (Kuhanek and Watling 2010). Some people with autism can experience hypo-sensitivity – an under-reaction of the senses. This can also change in relation to a person's emotional state, affect one or all senses and be interchangeable with hyper-sensitivity at any given time.

In addition to hyper- and hypo-sensitivity, autistic people may have other sensory perception difficulties. Objects and faces may appear distorted or sounds can be scrambled, making it hard for them to hear or distinguish what another person is saying when others are also talking (Bogdashina 2003). It is important to remember that all autistic people are unique and each person's sensory profile will be different. Furthermore, some autistic people may be aware of the impact of their sensory difficulties and able to successfully use their own strategies to manage them; others may be finding out about their differences for the first time and may continue to need much support in this area. Autistic people can also experience sensory overload, particulary when exposed to too much information. The National Autistic Society's (2017b) 'Can you make it to the end? Too much information' video demonstrates this experience.

Sensory difficulties can manifest in a variety of behavioural responses, some of which may be perceived as challenging. Much emphasis has been placed on preventative approaches, rather than reactive management, when working with individuals who present with challenging behaviours (Mansell 2007). A sensory profile can enable the occupational therapist to offer adaptive techniques to autistic people to help them modulate their behavioural responses, in contrast to simply managing their symptoms and not the cause. We have found making an initial assessment of an individual's sensory needs to be a crucial step in the support we offer so that they can have opportunities to acquire the higher-level skills they often want and need.

Adolescent/Adult Sensory Profile™

The Adolescent/Adult Sensory Profile (Brown and Dunn 2002) is a self-assessment questionnaire containing 60 items that describe responses to everyday sensory experiences. Autistic people complete the questionnaire by indicating the frequency of a response (almost never, seldom, occasionally, frequently, almost always) to various sensory experiences. The time needed to complete the questionnaire varies according to how much support an individual needs in making sense of the items; some may be read as double negatives, which are difficult for some autistic people to understand. The sensory profile is a visual non-intrusive tool, considered to be person-centred because it includes the individual in their assessment and intervention process, and clearly links their sensory processing to everyday experiences. Sensory differences may make engaging in activities difficult, thus creating a barrier to their independence. For this reason, it is vital to establish approaches that allow them to engage in activities of their choice so that they can work towards greater levels of independence. Sensory difference is thus a key area for assessment within autism; if not effectively assessed and supported, a person's quality of life may be severely reduced as sensory differences affect not just how someone lives and experiences the world but can also have a major impact upon their behaviour.

The Adolescent/Adult Sensory Profile™ helps the occupational therapist to identify the sensory processing patterns of people with autism and the effects they have on their functional performance. This tool is used, first, to gain information potentially vital to forming a better understanding of an individual's sensory processing patterns. Because some autistic people will struggle to understand why they engage in particular behaviours and/or why they prefer certain experiences or environments, the self-assessment questionnaire can result in the individual gaining an increased awareness and understanding of their sensory processing preferences as well as the occupational therapist. The information may also be useful for their family and others who may be involved in their care. Second, the tool enables more informed intervention planning, taking into account the individual's preferences. In intervention planning, it is important that sensory processing be considered within the context of what the individual needs or wants to do in their life; for example, we may use the information to request reasonable accommodations in the workplace – as shown below in the case of Shaun.

The scoring and interpretation of sensory profiles are based on Dunn's (2001) model, which focuses on the impact of sensory processing on a person's daily life. The concept behind the model is that a person's responses to sensory stimuli are informed by a combination of their sensory threshold (high and low) and the way in which they respond (passive or active). The sensory profile divides sensory processing into four quadrants: low registration, sensation seeking, sensation avoiding and sensory sensitivity. Low registration is a combination of high thresholds and passive responding; sensation seeking is a combination of high thresholds and active responding; sensory sensitivity is a combination of low thresholds and passive responding; and sensation avoiding is a combination of low thresholds and active responding (Dunn 1999, 2001). Many of the autistic people we see describe sensory processing differences and the impact these have on managing their daily life. Identifying such differences is vital to understanding how autistic adults experience daily life, and how their sensory experiences inform their behaviour and response to their world. This will now be explored through the case of Shaun.

> Shaun, aged 27, is employed by his local supermarket but has been struggling at work for the past few months due to high levels of anxiety and depression; as a result he has been signed off by his doctor. He wants to get back to work. His sensory profile identified high scores on low registration and withdrawal from the environment (sensation avoiding) in his auditory processing. It is essential that we consider Shaun's pattern of auditory processing and the effect this will have on him in the work environment. It is likely that due to his high score on low registration he will be slow to process verbal instructions and may miss some of what he is told. His high scores on sensation avoiding and sensory sensitivity will require equal consideration. He becomes overwhelmed when exposed to lots of noise and sounds that irritate him. Furthermore, he tends to avoid auditory

input thus increasing his risk of missing necessary information. ? scores on sensation seeking, meaning he is unlikely to pursue auditory s

Given these complex findings, Shaun will have difficulty distinguish taking in and using auditory information. He will benefit greatly from consistency in training and supervision. Increasing consistency increases predictability for Shaun, which decreases the information processing load thus making it easier for him to pick out the relevant information. This change in the work environment would also support Shaun's sensation avoiding preference because it incorporates structure and ritual. He may also derive benefit from a consistent work schedule and dealing with the same supervisor. Another possible change that could help Shaun is scheduling his shifts for less busy periods to reduce the overall sensory stimuli he is exposed to in the supermarket. He needs to be given information in multiple modalities, with limited auditory instructions, and supported by visual cues and practice. He also needs his tasks to be written down and specific tasks to be demonstrated. Shaun will benefit from working alongside another person while he is learning new tasks and being given opportunities to clarify instructions. He should be asked to demonstrate tasks or repeat instructions to ensure he has understood them. His supervisor may wish to consider making his work environment free from unnecessary distractions. Shaun will need support to get to know his colleagues; he will also benefit from being provided with a buddy with whom to share regular scheduled breaks. He will need to know who to go to when he feels overwhelmed.

This scenario validates the role of occupational therapists in helping autistic people to engage in and sustain work-related activities. They can educate employers about the sensory needs of people with autism, and provide key information about how to make the work environment more suitable for particular individuals. It is thought that only 15 per cent of adults with an ASC are in paid employment compared to 48 per cent of people with general disabilities (Department of Health 2009a). A great number of people with autism want to work and could do so if they were able to access appropriate support.

Equipment trialled within the specialist Enablement intervention

In the following subsections we describe our use of various types of equipment that have been used to help autistic adults gain greater independence.

ndicate an individual's need for *deep pressure*. One
/n people with autism, Temple Grandin, author
2014) and *Thinking in Pictures* (1995), described
and needing lots of heavy blankets on the bed
e ultimately designed a 'squeeze machine' that
: which worked as a form of stress relief therapy.
Grandin suggests that deep pressure and weighted blankets are of
benefit to some people with autism as these can have the same calming
effect. The benefits of deep pressure and hug stimulation are supported
by research (Edelson *et al.* 1999). Hugs release oxytocin (National
Institutes of Health 2007), a hormone that acts on the part of the brain
that deals with emotion and motivation. When oxytocin is released
it makes us feel good; for example, when we are close to loved ones,
including pets. It lowers levels of stress (anxiety) in the body, reduces
blood pressure and improves mood. It also seems to play an important
role in our relationships; that is, it has been linked to how much we
trust others, which is often a problematic issue for those with autism.

Weighted blankets and jackets have been trialled with those
whose sensory profile indicates that deep pressure and weighted
therapy may be of benefit. Weighted therapy items are matched to the
individual's body weight following consultation with the individual's
general practitioner to check that there are no contraindications (such
as epilepsy, circulatory/respiratory problems or physical difficulties)
that may prevent the person being able to use or remove the weighted
item. These safety concerns require equal consideration. We have
trialled these items with autistic adults over the age of 18 who are
able to communicate with us should they find the blanket/jacket
uncomfortable, painful or upsetting and are able to remove such an
item on their own. Parker and Koscinski (2016) found some reports
suggesting that the beneficial effects of a weighted item can be felt
within three to five minutes; indeed, some of our users have reported
feeling different immediately. Guidelines suggesting 20 minutes of
maximum exposure (L'Ordre des Ergothèrapeutes du Quèbec (OEQ)
2008) have not been accepted by the Alberta College of Occupational
Therapists Adhoc Task Force (2009) because the individual's tolerance
to the item and its potential benefits should guide such. A survey
involving over 300 occupational therapists (Parker n.d.) found that
most felt that blanket use should be based on the preference of the

person utilising it. This is the approach we have taken with weighted items. While we identified few studies supporting the effects of weighted items, Mullen *et al.* (2008) found that some adults who had trialled weighted blankets reported feeling less anxious and more relaxed. Our own anecdotal evidence supports this finding:

> *I feel grounded when using my weighted jacket. I felt like I was floating away before.*
>
> *My blanket has become part of me; I cannot sleep without it. I wake up feeling refreshed, a feeling I have not ever experienced.*
>
> *With my weighted jacket I can now go into shops without feeling so anxious.*
>
> *I am not sure what has happened but it's positive as I feel different, calmer.*
>
> *The blanket is not helping me sleep, but relaxing me so I can sleep; my thoughts are not racing around anymore, which was stopping me getting to sleep.*

Noise-cancelling headphones

Another sensory difference that commonly affects autistic people is hypersensitivity to noise. Noises can be magnified and sounds distorted and muddled. They may not be able to hear conversations in the distance or to filter out background noises. This hypersensitivity can often lead to further difficulties and frustrations, which impact all areas of their life. For some individuals, this difficulty has been a major obstacle to accessing opportunities that most people may take for granted.

One approach to managing this sensory difficulty is wearing *noise-cancelling headphones*. Subject to an individual's sensory profile we may recommend such if traditional headphones have not been effective. For some people these have been life-changing, as this carer's words demonstrate:

> *I just wanted to say a huge thank you for supplying Lenard with his noise-cancelling headphones. You cannot imagine the difference these have made to his daily life. They helped him avoid having a complete meltdown on a flight this summer when a very distressed baby sitting right next to us cried and screamed continually. Usually this would have caused Lenard unbelievable distress, but, although still very anxious, he was able to deal with it. He has also been able to attempt some situations he would usually be unable to cope with because he knows he has the ability to block out the noises he is so over-sensitive to at the flick of a button. Thank you so much for all the help you have given us. I can't begin to say how much we appreciate it.*

Visual aids

In addition to weighted items and noise-cancelling headphones, the occupational therapist may consider providing practical adaptive techniques, such as the use of *visual aids/prompts*. Activities of daily living need to be taught explicitly to some people with autism because they may not pick them up intuitively. Activities such as showering, preparing and cooking meals, cleaning, shopping and travelling on public transport are all adaptive skills. They are considered essential to adulthood and difficulty accomplishing them can considerably reduce an individual's ability to live independently. Duncan and Bishop (2013) found that half of the adolescents with high-functioning autism in their study demonstrated daily living skills that were significantly below expectation for someone of their age and intellectual ability. A quarter scored in the low range of adaptive functioning; in other words, their adaptive skills matched those of someone with mild to moderate intellectual disability. This study highlighted the need for such skills to be addressed before transition into adulthood if these people are expected to be able to live independently.

While visual aids have been used successfully with children, we have found that many of the autistic adults with whom we work also continue to prefer using them, regardless of intellect. Temple Grandin (1995, p. 14) promotes the use of visual aids, stating 'Spatial words such as over and under had no meaning for me until I had a visual image to fix them in my memory.'

We have found that visual aids have enabled many autistic adults to make sense of abstract concepts, such as how something should look. For example, following a visual recipe makes that experience more concrete, as does using photographs of their own kitchen appliances to teach them how to use those appliances in general. Although there is no one best way to support adults with autism, we have found visual aids – personalised to reflect each individual's unique circumstances, needs and wishes – most successful. More progress is made when information is concrete and visual and the individual practises the tasks they wish to learn. Visual aids are in line with the visual learning styles within which many people with autism work best. Grandin (cited in Boucher and Lewis 1989, pp. 99–122) states that she still has difficulty processing long strings of verbal information and has to write down verbal directions containing more than three steps. We often have to help autistic adults remember the sequence of a set of instructions, and have thus gained some valuable feedback on how visual aids can make them feel; for example:

> *Using the chart is making me feel more relaxed and I feel every time I move a picture along the strip I am achieving something. I also feel less emotional, which allows me to focus on the structured side of life…the practical…the doing, rather than the thinking.*
>
> *The photos are great because there is no language or words to confuse me!*

Telecare

Telecare refers to support and assistance provided at a distance using information and communication technology. It is the continuous, automatic and remote monitoring of its users by means of sensors to enable them to continue living in their home. Telecare can minimise the risk of fires, gas leaks and floods, and also deal with real-time emergencies. It can thus offer autistic people and their families and carers security and peace of mind. One of the simplest forms of telecare is a personal alarm, which consists of a button – often in the form of a pendant worn around the neck or on the wrist – and a base unit that works with the individual's landline. When the wearer pushes the pendant, their call is directed to a 24-hour monitoring centre staffed by trained operators who will answer their alarm call on any day of the year. Many autistic people can be vulnerable merely as a result of their autistic traits, such as taking people literally or being unable to imagine the consequences of their own or others' actions. Below are two examples of support offered by telecare:

> *Following the recent death of his mother, Charlie is now living on his own for the first time. He has experienced a few difficulties. First, he opened the front door to someone he did not know and believed her when she told him she had no money to feed her small child; he duly felt sorry for her and gave her a substantial amount of money. Charlie had little awareness of this caller's intention. Second, he is easily distracted by his Xbox and then forgets that he is midway through cooking dinner. The installation of a bogus caller button on his Telecare Lifeline unit – a small box that plugs into his landline – enabled him to automatically raise an alarm with the call centre should he fear answering the door to unwanted guests; the call centre can listen in to the conversation and intervene (and call the police, if necessary). Charlie now feels safer in his own home because he knows that he can access timely assistance. A smoke detector was also fitted. Telecare was also able to programme the unit with timed verbal prompts*

to remind Charlie to take his medication. Telecare serves to support Charlie and safeguard him from risks, thus enabling him to remain at home. He continues to live with minimal support.

Ann has an ASC and lives with her mother. She is reported to be aggressive. She also has generalised epilepsy, and her mother lies awake at night fearful that she will have a seizure. Ann wants to be independent and feels she has no quality of life because she has to leave her bedroom door open to allow her mother to watch over her. The installation of a bed sensor linked to her mother via a vibrating carer alert now allows Ann to keep her bedroom door closed and her mother to have a good night's sleep – she will be woken only in the event of Ann having a seizure. Ann's mum now reports that, since the installation of telecare support, Ann's aggressive behaviour has decreased and she is much happier.

Telecare continues to be an important source of risk reduction for autistic adults. It can promote their independence and also support the needs of the carer. In some cases telecare can reduce the need for a support package.

Phone apps

We have found a variety of apps to be useful in helping our clients to work toward and achieve goals; these include:

- *Local travel apps for trains and buses* – These can be helpful for learning to read timetables and plotting routes. They can help individuals to get to new places, attend appointments and access community activities.

- *Cooking apps* – These enable clients to follow recipes in pictorial, sequenced steps. They show cooking times and how something should look at each stage, and provide shopping lists for the necessary ingredients.

- *Anxiety-management apps* – Some of these help with anxiety, instantly using calming breathing exercises and other strategies to change the individual's focus. Others take the form of toolkits, which provide a variety of tools in one single app, such as coping tools (coping card, activity planner), inspirational quotes and distraction and relaxation activities, which can be personalised and help individuals become more aware of how to self-regulate their physical and emotional responses.

- *Budgeting apps* – These have also been found to be useful, in particular those that support daily budgeting (transactions) and/or manage the individual's regular income, recurring expenses and savings. We have used these in place of or in addition to paper versions in response to individual preference.

- *Mindfulness apps* – These have proved helpful in supporting some individuals to track their mood, health and thoughts, thus enabling them to be more self-aware and to notice patterns and trends. The relaxation activities and mindfulness meditation offered on these apps can be used to help clients learn techniques to better manage their stress, anxiety and/or depression. Some provide additional support whereby clients can connect with others who are experiencing the same difficulties, together with daily prompts to check in with how one is feeling.

- *Weather apps* – These are useful for clients who struggle to select appropriate clothing for the weather. This information will enable them to better plan their day. Weather apps may often be used with a prompt from a visual routine board. A visual routine board is used to provide additional structure and an overview of activities. Activities can be organised on a daily or weekly basis, and broken down further into specific times of the day at which more visual supports are needed. For example, the autistic person may have no awareness of what clothes to wear in relation to the weather and thus select shorts and a T-shirt when rain is forecast. A photograph, symbol, written word/s or a picture can act as a prompt to check their weather app and then to select the correct clothes for the day in question. Alternatively, a daily alarm can be set on their phone to prompt them to check the weather. Visual routine boards and visual supports have been highly welcomed by many of our autistic clients. For example, Kevin, who has a PhD, uses a visual aid (in this case, a sequence of pictorial steps) to cook meals for his family, something he was not able to do prior to his Enablement intervention.

- *Medication prompt apps* – These are a good resource should an individual require prompting to take, order and manage their own medication.

We have found these apps the most successful but nevertheless continue to explore others with our clients; indeed, often it is clients themselves who find them. The Apps market continues to grow and many of the offerings are free to use.

Facebook and other social groups

Our service has its own Enablement page on Facebook as we have found that many of our clients use social media as a way of communicating with others. Many individuals persistently report their continued difficulties in forming friendships and state that they need to rehearse or prepare for face-to-face social situations. This can frequently put our clients under extreme stress, further reducing their opportunities to engage with others and experience positive friendships. Unfortunately, lack of friendship can result in low self-esteem, anxiety and depression (Hay, Payne, and Chadwick 2004). Occupational therapists have shown how Facebook can facilitate positive friendships and how adults can be supported to access the wider community through age-related meaningful activities (Gasson and Cruse 2013). Kent County Council has also commissioned ASC peer support groups, which have been successful in facilitating additional opportunities for clients to meet regularly to widen their social networks and enhance their social inclusion, health and well-being through increased social interaction.

To conclude this chapter, we have highlighted the value of occupational therapy interventions; discussed person-centred, measurable goals and outcomes within a specialist Enablement intervention; and described the tools, assessment and equipment we have trialled as part of our Enablement research.

Bibliography

Abbeduto, L., Seltzer, M., Shattuck, P., and Krauss, M. (2004) 'Psychological well-being and coping in mothers of youths with autism, Down syndrome, or fragile X syndrome.' *American Journal of Mental Retardation* 109, 237–254.

Abell, F. and Hare, D. (2005) 'Experimental investigation of the phenomenology of delusional beliefs in people with Aspergers syndrome.' Accessed on 28/04/2017 at www.journals.sagepub.com/doi/abs/10.1177/1362361305057857.

American Occupational Therapy Association (2010) 'The scope of occupational therapy services for individuals with an autism spectrum disorder across the life course.' *American Journal of Occupational Therapy* 64 (suppl.), 125–136.

Alberta College of Occupational Therapy Adhoc Task Force (2009) *Commentary on l'Ordre des Ergothèrapeutes du Quèbec Position Statement on Use of Weighted Covers* [out of circulation].

Ayres, J. (1979) *Sensory Integration and the Child*. Torrance, CA: Western Psychological Services.

Ayres, J. (2005) *Sensory Integration and the Child: Understanding Hidden Sensory Challenges*, 25th anniversary edition, revised and updated by Pediatric Therapy Network. Los Angeles, CA: WPS.

Bancroft, K., Batten, A., Lambert, S., and Madders, T. (2012) *The Way We Are: Autism in 2012*. London: National Autistic Society.

Baranek, G. (2002) 'Efficacy of sensory and motor interventions for children with autism.' *Journal of Autism and Developmental Disorders* 32, 5, 397–422.

Beardon, L. and Edmonds, G. (2007) 'ASPECT consultancy report: A national report on the needs of adults with Asperger syndrome.' Accessed on 06/08/2017 at www.sheffield.ac.uk/polopoly_fs/1.34791!/file/ASPECT_Consultancy_report.pdf.

Billstedt, E., Gillberg, C., and Gillberg, C. (2005) 'Autism after adolescence: Population-based 13- to 22-year follow-up study of 120 individuals with autism diagnosed in childhood.' *Journal of Autism and Developmental Disorders* 35, 3, 351–360.

Bloomer, M. and Rose, C. (1989) *Frames of Reference Guiding Treatment for Children with Autism in Developmental Disabilities: A Handbook for Occupational Therapists*. London: Haworth Press.

Bogdashina, O. (2003) *Sensory Perceptual Issues in Autism: Different Sensory Experiences – Different Perceptual Worlds*. London: Jessica Kingsley Publishers.

Boucher, J. and Lewis, V. (1989) 'Memory impairments and communication in relatively able autistic children.' *Journal of Child Psychology and Psychiatry* 30, 99–122.

Bouma, R. and Schweitzer, R. (1990) 'The impact of chronic childhood illness on family stress: A comparison between autism and cystic fibrosis.' *Journal of Clinical Psychology* 46, 722–730.

Brown, C. and Dunn, W. (2002) *Adolescent/Adult Sensory Profile*. San Antonio, TX: PsychCorp.

Bruni, L. (2010) 'The dappiness of sociality.' *Economics and Eudaimonia, Rationality and Society* 22, 4, 383–406.

Burns, S. and MacKeith, J. (2012) *Spectrum Star*™. Triangle Consulting Social Enterprise Ltd. Accessed on 06/08/2017 at www.outcomesstar.org.uk.

Christiansen, C. and Townsend, E. (eds) (2004) *Introduction to Occupation: The Art and Science of Living*. Upper Saddle River, NJ: Prentice Hall.

Church, C., Alinsanski, S., and Amanullah, S (2000) 'The social, behavioural, and academic experiences of children with Asperger syndrome.' *Focus on Autism and Other Developmental Disabilities* 15, 12–20.

College of Occupational Therapists (2010a) *Position Statement. Reablement: The Added Value of Occupational Therapists*. London: College of Occupational Therapists.

College of Occupational Therapists (2010b) *Code of Ethics and Professional Conduct*. London: College of Occupational Therapists.

College of Occupational Therapists (2013) *Sensory Integration (Practice Briefing)*. London: College of Occupational Therapists.

College of Occupational Therapists (2015) *Measuring Outcomes (Research Briefing)*. London: College of Occupational Therapists.

College of Occupational Therapists (2017) *Professional Standards for Occupational Therapy Practice*. London: College of Occupational Therapists.

Cosby, J. and Johnston, S. (2010) 'Sensory processing disorders and social participation.' *American Journal of Occupational Therapy* 64, 3, 462–473.

Crane, L., Goddard, L., and Pring, L. (2009) 'Sensory processing in adults with autism spectrum disorders.' *Autism* 13, 3, 215–228.

Department of Health (2009a) *Valuing Employment Now.* London: Department of Health.

Department of Health (2009b) *A Better Future: A Consultation on a Future Strategy for Adults with Autistic Spectrum Disorders.* London: Department of Health.

Department of Health and Social Services Inspectorate (1995) *Carers (Recognition and Services) Act 1995.* London: HMSO.

Dilk, M. and Bond, G. (1996) 'Meta-analytic evaluation of skills training research for individuals with severe mental illness.' *Journal of Consulting and Clinical Psychology* 64, 6, 1337–1346.

Dumas, J., Wolf, L., Fishman, S., and Culligan, A. (1991) 'Parenting stress, child behaviour problems and dysphoria in parents of children with autism, Down syndrome, behaviour disorders and normal development.' *Exceptionality* 2, 97–110.

Duncan, A. and Bishop, S. (2013) 'Understanding the gap between cognitive abilities and daily living skills in adolescents with autism spectrum disorders with average intelligence.' *Autism.* Accessed on 06/08/2017 at http://journals.sagepub.com/doi/abs/10.1177/1362361313510068.

Duncan, E. (2006) *Foundations for Practice in Occupational Therapy,* 4th edition. London: Churchill Livingstone.

Dunn, W. (1999) *Sensory Profile.* San Antonio, TX: PsychCorp.

Dunn, W. (2001) 'The sensations of everyday life: Empirical, theoretical, and pragmatic considerations.' *American Journal of Occupational Therapy* 55, 6, 608–620.

Dunn, W., Myles, B., and Orr, S. (2002) 'Sensory processing issues associated with Asperger's syndrome: A preliminary investigation.' *American Journal of Occupational Therapy* 56, 97–102.

Edelson, S., Kerr, D., Edelson, M., Grandin, T. *et al.* (1999) 'Behavioural and physiological effects of deep pressure on children with autism: A pilot study evaluating the efficacy of Grandin's hug machine.' *American Journal of Occupational Therapy* 53, 2, 145–152.

European Network of Occupational Therapy in Higher Education Terminology Project Group (2004) 'Occupational Therapy terminology database.' Accessed on 28/04/2017 at www.enothe.eu.

Fisher, A. (2009) *Occupational Therapy Intervention Process Model: A Model for Planning and Implementing Top-down, Client-centered, and Occupational-based Occupational Therapy Interventions.* Fort Collins, CO: Three Star Press.

Fisher, A. and Bray Jones, K. (2010) *Assessment of Motor and Process Skills.* Volume 1: *Development, Standardization, and Administration Manual,* 7th edition. Fort Collins, CO: Three Star Press.

Forsyth, K. Salamy, M., Simon, S., and Kielhofner, G. (1998) *A User's Guide to the Assessment of Communication and Interaction Skills (ACIS),* Version 4.0. Chicago, IL: University of Illinois.

Galanopoulos, A., Robertson, D., Spain, D., and Murphy, C. (2014) 'Mental health and autism – depression, anxiety and OCD.' *Your Autism Magazine,* Mental Health Supplement 8, 4, Winter.

Gasson, S. and Cruse, W. (2013) 'The importance of friendship: Activities feature.' *Occupational Therapy News* July, p. 43.

Glendinning, C., Jones, K., Baxter, K., Rabiee, P. *et al.* (2010) *Home Care Re-ablement Services: Investigating the Longer-term Impacts (Prospective Longitudinal Study).* York and Canterbury: Social Policy Research Unit and Personal Social Services Research Unit.

Grandin, T. (1995) *Thinking in Pictures and Other Reports from My Life with Autism* (p. 30). New York: Doubleday.

Grandin, T. (2006) *Thinking in Pictures: My Life with Autism*. New York: Vintage.

Grandin, T. (2014) *The Autistic Brain*. London: Rider.

Grandin, T. and Scariano, M. (1986) *Emergence: Labelled Autistic*. Navato, CA: Arena Press.

Greenblatt, M., Becerra, R., and Serafetinides, E. (1982) 'Social networks and mental health: An overview.' *American Journal of Psychiatry* 139, 8, 977–984.

Graetz, J. (2010) 'Autism grows up: Opportunities for adults with autism.' *Disability and Society* 25, 33–47.

Håkansson, C., Dahlin, S., and Sonn, U. (2006) 'Achieving balance in everyday life.' *Journal of Occupational Science* 13, 1, 74–82.

Hamilton, D., Sherman, S., and Lickel, B. (2005) 'Perceiving social groups: The importance of the entitativity continuum.' In D.L. Hamilton (ed.) *Social Cognition: Key Readings in Social Psychology* (pp. 405–419). Secaicus, NJ: Psychology Press.

Hay, D.M., Payne, A., and Chadwick, A. (2004) 'Peer relations in childhood.' *Journal of Child Psychology and Psychiatry* 45, 1, 84–108.

Heffernan, D. (2016) *Sensory Issues for Adults with Autism Spectrum Disorder*. London: Jessica Kingsley Publishers.

Howlin, P., Goode, S., Hutton, J., and Rutter, M. (2004) 'Adult outcome for children with autism.' *Journal of Child Psychology and Psychiatry* 45, 212–229.

Hudson, B. (2010) 'An asset-based approach to community building.' Surrey Community Care. Accessed on 28/04/2017 at www.communitycare.co.uk/06/11/an-asset-based-approach- to-community-building.

Jasmin, E., Couture, M., McKinley, P., and Reid, G. (2009) 'Sensori-motor and daily living skills of preschool children with autistic spectrum disorder.' *Journal of Autism and Developmental Disorders* 39, 2, 231–241.

Kielhofner, G. (ed.) (2008) *Model of Human Occupation: Theory and Application*, 4th edition. Baltimore: Lippincott Williams & Wilkins.

Kielhofner, G. and Neville, A. (1983) 'The modified interest checklist.' Unpublished manuscript, University of Illinois at Chicago.

Koenig, K. and Kinnealey, M. (2010) 'Adults with an autism spectrum disorder.' In H. Miller-Kuhaneck and R. Watling (eds) *Autism: A Comprehensive Occupational Therapy Approach*, 3rd edition. White Plains, MD: AOTA Press.

Kopelowicz, A., Liberman, R.P., and Zarate, R. (2006) 'Recent advances in social skills training for schizophrenia.' *Schizophrenia Bulletin* 32, 1, S12–S23.

Kramer, J., Kielhofner, G., and Forsyth, K. (2007) 'Assessments used with the Model of Human Occupation.' In B.J. Hemphill-Pearson (ed.) *Assessments in Occupational Therapy Mental Health*, 2nd edition (pp. 159–184). Therofare, NJ: Slack Incorporated.

Krupa, T., Woodside, H., and Pocock, K (2010) 'Activity and social participation in the period following a first episode of psychosis and implications for occupational therapy.' *British Journal of Occupational Therapy* 73, 1, 13–20.

Kuhanek, H. and Watling, R. (2010) *Autism: A Comprehensive Occupational Therapy Approach*. Bethesda, MD: American Occupational Therapy Association.

Law, M. (2005) 'Measurement in occupational therapy.' In M. Law, C. Baum and W. Dunn (eds) *Measuring Occupational Performance*, 2nd edition (pp. 3–20). Thorofare, NJ: Slack Incorporated.

Mansell, J. (2007) *Services for People with Learning Disability and Challenging Behaviour or Mental Health Needs*. London: Department of Health.

Mawhood, L.M., Howlin, P., and Rutter, M. (2000) 'Autism and developmental receptive language disorder: A follow-up comparison in early adult life – cognitive and language outcomes.' *Journal of Child Psychology and Psychiatry* 41, 561–565.

Mayes, S., Calhoun, S., Mayes, D., and Molitoris, S. (1999) 'Autism and ADHD: Overlapping and discriminating symptoms.' *Research in Autism Spectrum Disorders* 6, 1, 277–285.

Mesibov, G. (1983) 'Current perspectives and issues in autism and adolescence.' In E. Schopler and G.B. Mesibov (eds) *Autism in Adolescents and Adults* (pp. 37–53). New York: Plenum Press.

Mesibov, G. and Handlan, S. (1997) 'Adolescents and adults with autism.' In D.J. Cohen and F.R. Volkmar (eds) *Handbook of Autism and Pervasive Developmental Disorders*, 2nd edition (pp. 309–322). New York: Wiley.

Mickel, A. (2010) 'Rethinking reablement.' *Occupational Therapy News* 18, 11, 36–37.

Montes, G. and Halterman, J.S. (2007) 'Psychological functioning and coping among mothers of children with autism: A population-based study.' *Pediatrics* 119, 1040–1046.

Mullen, B., Champagne, T., Krishnamurty, S., Dickson, D. *et al.* (2008) 'Exploring the safety and therapeutic effects of deep pressure stimulation using a weighted blanket.' *Occupational Therapy in Mental Health* 24, 65–89.

National Autistic Society (2007) *Autism and Independence. A Guide for Local Authorities: Enabling Adults with an Autism Spectrum Disorder to Achieve Greater Independence.* London: National Autistic Society.

National Autistic Society (2017a) 'About autism.' Accessed on 13/1/2017 at www.autism.org.uk/about/what-is/asd.aspx.

National Autistic Society (2017b) 'Can you make it to the end? Too much information.' YouTube video. Accessed on 01/06/2017 at www.youtube.com/watch?v=Lr4_dOorquQ.

National Health Service Information Centre (2012). *Estimating the Prevalence of Autism Spectrum Conditions in Adults: Extending the 2007 Adult Psychiatric Morbidity Survey.* Leeds: National Health Service Information Centre for Health and Social Care.

National Institutes of Health (NIH) (2007) 'NIH news in health.' Accessed on 12/12/2016 at https://newsinhealth.nih.gov/2007/february/docs/01features_01.htm.

Nicholson, D. and Kerslake, B. (2011) *£162m Additional Winter Pressures to Primary Care Trusts* (letter). London: Department of Health.

Oakley, F., Kielhofner, G., Barris, R., and Reichter, R. (1986) 'The role checklist: Development and empirical assessment of reliability.' *Occupational Therapy Journal of Research* 6, 3, 157–169.

O'Neill, J. (1999) *Through the Eyes of Aliens: A Book about Autistic People.* London: Jessica Kingsley Publishers.

Ordre des ergothèrapeutes du Quèbec (2008) 'OEQ position statement on the use of weighted covers.' Accessed on 28/04/2017 at https://cotbc.org/wp-content/uploads/OEQPositionStatement_WeightedCovers.pdf.

Parker, E. (n.d.) 'OT weighted blanket survey.' Accessed on 17/02/2107 at www.eileenparker.com/ot-weighted-blanket-survey.

Parker, E. and Koscinski, C. (2016) *The Weighted Blanket Guide.* London: Jessica Kingsley Publishers.

Rabiee, P. and Glendinning, C. (2011) 'Organisation and delivery of home care re-ablement: What makes a difference?' *Health and Social Care in the Community* 19, 5, 495–503.

Riley, J. (2012) *The Effectiveness of Occupational Therapy Local Authority Social Services' Interventions for Older People in Great Britain: A Critical Literature Review.* London: College of Occupational Therapists.

Seltzer, M., Greenberg, J., Hong, J., Smith, L.E. *et al.* (2010) 'Maternal cortisol levels and behaviour problems in adolescents and adults with ASD.' *Journal of Autism and Developmental Disorders* 40, 457–469.

Social Care Institute for Excellence (2010) *Reablement: Emerging Practice Messages.* London: Social Care Institute for Excellence.

Social Services Improvement Agency (2011) *Demonstrating Improvement from Reablement: Phase 1 Overview Report.* Cardiff: Welsh Assembly.

Trombly, C. (1995) 'The 1995 Eleanor Clarke Slagle lecture. Occupation: Purposefulness and meaningfulness as therapeutic mechanisms.' *American Journal of Occupational Therapy* 49, 10, 960–972.

Vermeulen, P. (2012) *Autism as Context Blindness.* Lenexa, KS: AAPC Publishing.

Volkmar, F. and Kiln, A. (1995) 'Social developments in autism: Historical and clinical perspectives.' In S. Baron-Cohen, H. Tager-Flusberg and D. Cohen (eds) *Understanding Other Minds: Perspectives from Autism* (pp. 40–55). New York: Oxford University Press.

Wilcock, A. (1993) 'A theory of the human need for occupation.' *Journal of Occupational Science* 1, 1, 17–24.

Williams, D. (1999) *Nobody Nowhere.* London: Jessica Kingsley Publishers.

Williams, M.S. and Shellenberger, S. (1996) *'How Does Your Engine Run?'® A Leader's Guide to the Alert Program for Self-regulation.* Albuquerque, NM: Therapy Works, Inc.

World Federation of Occupational Therapists (2016) 'Definition occupation.' Accessed on 02/05/2017 at www.wfot.org/AboutUs/AboutOccupationalTherapy/DefinitionofOccupationalTherapy.aspx.

Chapter 4

Specialist Enablement Research Results and Analysis

Ute Vann and Sandra Gasson

This chapter explores and analyses our research findings. It then provides three case studies illustrating these findings. The findings are related to the following measuring tools:

- Spectrum Star™

- Exit interview with research participants (week 12)

- Carers' questionnaire and self-esteem questionnaire

- Enablement resource analysis

- Cost-setting analysis

Separate from the above five measurements, the occupational therapist also completed assessments of motor processing skills (AMPS) with 20 participants, the results of which are presented together with some vignettes of personal outcomes and three more detailed case studies.

Research results

Measurements for the research project were taken in three stages: at week one of the specialist Enablement intervention. (*Note:* week one was technically the start of the Enablement intervention itself but the five measurements were, of course, taken slightly earlier by the original assessing case manager.) The next measurement was taken at week 12, when specialist Enablement ended. The final measurement added a longitudinal element by occurring 12 weeks post-intervention, at week 24; it was intended to measure whether longer-term benefits resulted from the intervention.

Some basics

Thirty-six individuals signed up to the intervention, of whom 30 (83 per cent) completed the programme; at the third stage (week 24), 23 (64 per cent) were still part of the project. At all stages, the proportion of males to females was almost equal but there were significant differences in the age ranges.

Participant profiles at weeks 1, 12 and 24, by age and gender

Table 4.1 shows that the males in the youngest age group comprised 75 per cent of participants. The opposite was true for the older age groups; that is, females accounted for 75 per cent of participants. Fifty-five per cent of those who joined the research project were aged 18–24 years (which reflects the age profile of all referrals to the ASC Team).

Males and females left the programme early in equal numbers. However, people in the 18–24 age group were most likely to leave early.

Individuals gave various reasons for leaving the specialist Enablement intervention early (before week 12), including: becoming mentally unwell, no longer wanting to engage, not wanting to be assessed again, feeling that they had benefitted enough and, in one case, the carer of the individual had problems of their own and the individual felt unable to continue without them. Withdrawal at later stages was for two reasons: not wanting to be assessed again, and a change in circumstances (between weeks 12 and 24), including moving home, attending college or looking for work.

Participants were overwhelmingly of white ethnicity. Thirty-five individuals were recorded as having a white background, and one individual classed themselves as white and black Caribbean. These figures reflect the picture in general, in that the vast majority of referrals to the ASC Team are for individuals with white backgrounds.

Of the initial 36 participants, 28 lived with their family and 8 lived independently. This was true for all age groups. Interestingly, only 17 carers chose/agreed to respond to the carers' questionnaire at the beginning of the intervention. All were primary carers.

When looking at the time of diagnosis of the 36 individuals signing up for the research project, significant differences emerged between males and females, as shown in Figures 4.1 and 4.2. The

Table 4.1 Age and gender of participants

Participants	Gender		Age					
			18–24		25–40		41–54	
	Male	Female	Male	Female	Male	Female	Male	Female
Week 1 – 36	19	17	15	5	4	9	–	3
Week 12 – 30	15	15	12	4	3	8	–	3
Week 24 – 23	12	11	9	2	3	6	–	3

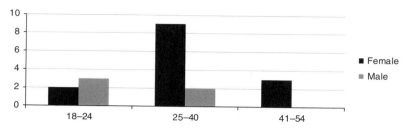

Figure 4.1 Diagnosed less than two years ago

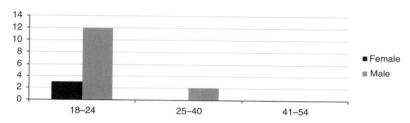

Figure 4.2 Diagnosed more than two years ago

vast majority of female participants were diagnosed within the last two years and the reverse was true for males. For males, it is more likely that they were diagnosed as children and adolescents. This is in line with research indicating that many females are diagnosed later in life. According to Mills and Kenyon (2013, p. 5), 'females with social and communication disorders may be much more likely to attract alternative diagnoses...in the absence of gender-sensitive protocol'.

A significant number of the 36 individuals signing up for the research project had diagnosed co-morbidities: 14 (38 per cent) had clinical depression; 7 had obsessive compulsive disorder (OCD) and 7 also had other long-term mental health conditions; and 6 had attention deficit hyperactivity disorder (ADHD). In comparison, relatively few had physical health conditions.

Results from Spectrum Star™

The ASC Team received help with analysing the results from the Outcomes Star™ developer, Triangle Consulting. The star is marketed as being 'underpinned by a model of change', and is a self-assessment tool which individuals use to rate the impact of key aspects of autism in the areas of:

- Communication
- Living skills and self-care
- Physical health
- Relationships
- Sensory differences
- Social skills
- Socially responsible behaviour
- Time and activities
- Well-being and self-esteem

Individuals rate themselves on a scale from 1 to 10 based on descriptions of what the different scores mean with regard to needing support in the particular area. The higher the score, the more independent an individual is in that area; the lower the score, the more support the individual needs in that area. The scores are categorised as follows:

- Choice and self-reliance, 9–10
- Learning for yourself, 7–8
- Stable, 5–6
- Accepting some support, 3–4
- Autism is a major barrier, 1–2

These stages describe the individual's progression through a 'journey of change' during a particular intervention. In the case of specialist Enablement, the following overall changes were self-assessed by the participants. Of the 23 participants who were measured at all three stages, overall, 61% of those who assessed themselves to be within the 1–2 range moved to 3–4; 81% of those who assessed themselves to be within the 3–4 range moved to 5–6; 53% of those assessing themselves to be within the 5–6 range moved to 7–8; and 19% of those assessing themselves to be within the 7–8 range moved to 9–10. Overall, the research sample, on average, started at 6 and above in one area only – 'Socially responsible behaviour' – and finished at 6 or above in every area except 'Time and activities'. The research appears to suggest that the individuals involved in specialist Enablement had a significant level of insight into the factors that had a negative impact on their lives. The overall successes can be summarised as follows:

- On average, 83% of participants improved in all areas; 100% improved in more than one area; and 91% improved in at least two areas.

- The highest areas of improvement over the 24-week period were 'Living skills and self-care', at an average of 2.3 points + change for all final measurements, and 'Sensory differences' at 2.03 (unsurprisingly, considering the provision was led by occupational therapists).

- The areas with the greatest percentage of individuals assessing themselves as having significant needs were 'Well-being and Self-esteem', 'Social skills' and 'Time and activities' (more than 85% started at 1–6).

- The 'Relationships' and 'Communication' areas showed the smallest percentage of improving and relatively low mean change.

Results for weeks 1–12 (Enablement period)

This period was key to our analysis because we are essentially assessing the benefit of the 12 weeks of direct Enablement support. Table 4.2 displays the statistics for the 30 individuals who completed the provision and all measurements.

Any change of 2.00 and higher is considered highly significant. Clearly, the changes in 'Living skills and self-care' and 'Well-being and self-esteem' were scored highest. These results are easily explained: most goals were set in these areas and they also lend themselves naturally to an occupational therapy approach. There was also clearly a knock-on effect for other areas, supporting the hypothesis that the goal/task-based approach works well for this client group; that is, an increase in functional skills in one area, such as daily living, might also improve an individual's sense of well-being. Specialist Enablement worked on specific goals/tasks but also provided more holistic support, such as improving ability to manage time and activities, and specialist help to integrate sensory preferences. It is also positive to note that the lowest

Table 4.2 Results for weeks 1–12

All 30 service users	Week 1	Week 12	Change
All areas	5.04	6.40	1.36
Physical health	5.40	6.00	*0.60*
Living skills and self-care	4.50	6.50	**2.00**
Well-being and self-esteem	4.03	5.80	**1.77**
Sensory differences	4.30	5.67	1.37
Communication	5.37	6.83	1.46
Social skills	4.53	5.97	1.44
Relationships	5.27	6.40	1.13
Socially responsible behaviour	7.67	8.45	*0.78*
Time and activities	4.30	5.97	1.67

Note: Italic = lowest; bold = highest.

levels of change, those for 'Physical health' and 'Socially responsible behaviour', were already scored relatively highly at the onset of the intervention, that is, at week 1.

Results for weeks 1–24 (Enablement period plus 12-week longitudinal review)

The statistics for the 23 individuals included in this measurement are shown in Table 4.3 and described below.

The main improvement, as expected, is in the area of 'Living skills and self-care'. However, the next most-improved area for those who were still available for assessment at 24 weeks was 'Sensory differences'. There was a notable increase between weeks 12 and 24, from 1.37 to 2.09, for which no explanation can currently be given. (Clearly, at week 24 there were fewer individuals involved than at week 12.) One hypothesis is that the advanced sensory work – which is integral to the Enablement provision – has significant and sustained potential over time. This makes theoretic sense in that sensory integration forms the building blocks of development;

Table 4.3 Results for weeks 1–24

All 23 service users	Week 1	Week 24	Change
All areas	5.16	6.57	1.41
Physical health	5.39	6.74	1.35
Living skills and self-care	4.52	6.83	**2.31**
Well-being and self-esteem	4.00	5.87	1.87
Sensory differences	4.43	6.52	**2.09**
Communication	5.52	6.74	1.22
Social skills	4.61	6.22	1.61
Relationships	5.52	6.22	*0.70*
Socially responsible behaviour	8.04	8.57	*0.53*
Time and activities	4.39	5.48	1.09

Note: Italic = lowest; bold = highest.

if effective assessment, support and aids are provided for individuals, it is likely they will see improvement in this area beyond the duration of the Enablement intervention. These figures relate to only a very small sample of individuals; however, data collected from further specialist Enablement provision may show whether this is a consistent area of improvement.

Results from exit interview

The questionnaire was administered by the researchers at the end of the specialist Enablement intervention (at week 12). At this stage, 30 individuals had completed specialist Enablement and all of them responded to the questionnaire.

The questionnaire asked a mixture of open and semi-closed questions and the researchers ordered the responses by themes. The main results from this exercise are described below.

When asked what goals they had set themselves at the beginning of specialist Enablement, the majority of individuals stated that they wanted to organise activities (of everyday living) and to learn to

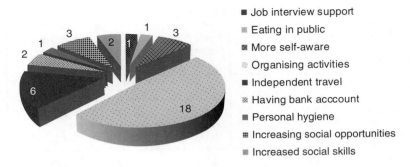

Figure 4.3 Goals set

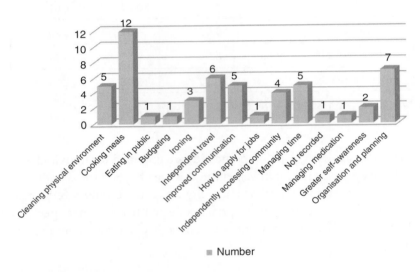

Figure 4.4 New skills learnt

travel independently (see Figure 4.3). Goals were worked on using a variety of approaches, including graded exposure, role modelling, establishment of strategies and routines and provision of practical support and guidance.

When asked what new skills they had learnt during the Enablement process, most participants indicated those related to practical activities within the home environment. Learning these skills, however, had also involved improvements in managing time, planning and/or organisational ability and communication (see Figure 4.4). The following observations were made during the course of the exit interviews:

I rationalise people's moods and body language. Focus on one thing at a time. Swim again.

I can manage my emotions better or at best understand them.

I can understand more why I find being around other people so hard, and have learnt ways to meet new people.

I can do meal planning by myself and then make a shopping list.

I am able to get to places via public transport and have the necessary knowledge to combat anxiety in social situations.

I actually finish things now where before I got distracted.

I can clean and maintain my home. I can cook simple meals using adapted recipes.

Other findings include:

- When individuals were asked what they felt was most beneficial about their specialist Enablement experience, most cited cooking guidance ($n = 7$), managing routines ($n = 7$), learning to travel independently ($n = 5$), emotional support ($n = 4$) and specialist knowledge of autism and what works for them ($n = 4$).

- When individuals were asked how specialist Enablement had helped them, most referred to guidance on how to carry out domestic activities ($n = 13$), feeling more confident about achieving goals ($n = 8$), feeling more in control of life ($n = 5$) and experiencing less social anxiety and increased social interaction ($n = 5$). Clearly, the beneficial effects of specialist Enablement went beyond merely learning a practical skill/activity.

- When asked about the longer-term benefits of specialist Enablement provision, 22 individuals cited learning and sustaining new skills and 7 said that they had more self-confidence.

- All 30 individuals said that they would recommend specialist Enablement. When asked why, most cited the encouragement to learn new skills, improved emotional well-being, practical help and greater self-awareness.

Participants made the following comments about their experience of the specialist Enablement intervention:

Someone to show me new ideas and ways of doing things, a new set of eyes and mind. Amazing and helpful to a point; it helped me get my life back on track and stopped me doing something that would end my own life.

I feel more enthusiastic to do stuff, doing things by myself.

Having someone who understands what life can be like and being able to help without it being overwhelming.

I feel more confident going to unfamiliar places.

I organise my life better; I am more confident about cooking and eating regularly.

I feel more confident now and better about myself.

Results from carers' questionnaire

Seventeen carers responded to this questionnaire, which was designed and had been used previously by Kent County Council. Since not all carers responded, the results cannot be generalised; however, this questionnaire still yielded valuable information.

Carer profile

- Of the 17 carers responding to the questionnaire, 15 were female. This result may indicate that women do most of the caring; however, it could also be the case that women were more willing to respond to the questionnaire than men.

- Sixteen carers were from an ethnically white background; one carer was of mixed-race heritage. This mirrors what is known about the participants in the specialist Enablement intervention.

- Seventy per cent of carers were aged between 41–60, which means that most of our participants were probably being supported by their parents.

- Of the 17 carers, 11 had mental health problems, physical disabilities or other long-term conditions.

- Just over half of carers were in full- or part-time employment; 6 were unemployed and 2 were retired.

- In response to being asked how much control they felt they had over their lives, none thought that they had no control whatsoever. Ten reported that they did not have as much control as they would like and 7 said that they had as much control as they wanted.

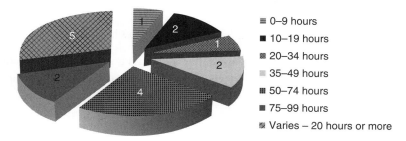

Figure 4.5 Weekly hours of care provided

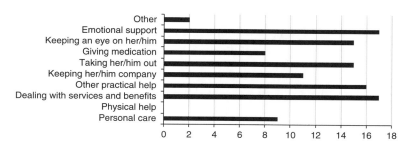

Figure 4.6 Care/support activities

Carers' responsibilities

Carers were asked to estimate how many hours of support they provided to the individual per week (see Figure 4.5). Of the 17 carers, 14 estimated that they provided more than 20 hours of support per week; of these 14, 6 thought that they provided more than 50 hours per week. When looking at what support was actually provided, the following activities were cited (see Figure 4.6). All carers named provision of emotional support and dealing with services and benefits. Most carers also provided practical help, took the individual out and kept them company/kept an eye on them. No carer provided physical support. The responses may reflect the fact that individuals participating in the specialist Enablement intervention were not in receipt of other support services. Some of the responses reflect the very particular difficulties of individuals on the autistic spectrum, such as anxiety about social interaction.

Other findings

The carers' questionnaire also revealed the following findings:

- Of the 17 carers, 11 said that they had some encouragement and support in their caring role but not enough and 6 said that they had no encouragement/support. The results appear to indicate that most carers, to some extent, felt not supported enough.

- Fifteen carers spend some time on things they value and enjoy but not enough. Only six felt that they had as much social contact with others as they wanted; nine had some contact but not enough; and two had no social contact and felt socially isolated. These results indicate that for most respondents the caring role has a significant impact on their social life.

- Eleven carers had used support services to obtain information and advice; 11 had received advice about carers' assessments and 10 had attended carers' groups or spoken to someone in confidence on a one-to-one basis. Three carers had not used a carer support service (at assessment by the ASC Team, all carers were advised about carers' support agencies and, where desired, were linked to them). These responses appear to indicate that most carers obtained support in the form of information rather than practical help with their caring responsibilities.

These results were reported to Kent County Council to inform provision of support for carers.

Results from self-esteem questionnaire

This questionnaire, developed by Rosenberg (1965), was administered at the beginning (week 1) and end (week 12) of the specialist Enablement intervention; it was effectively a self-assessed rating. Participants' scores were averaged and, overall, self-esteem was deemed to be 12 per cent higher by week 12. However, a note of caution should be added here: scores on the self-esteem questionnaire were those most affected by exterior forces/events/pressures. Life events and associated anxiety can alter the self-esteem of a person on the autistic spectrum significantly; indeed, an individual may record different scores at different times on the same day. For example, one participant's score

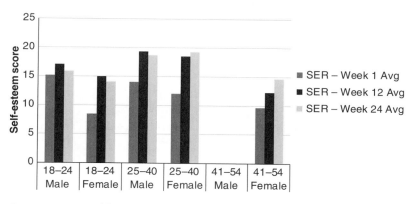

Figure 4.7 Average self-esteem at each assessment period

had decreased by the end of the intervention and we subsequently discovered that she had been issued with an eviction notice at that time, which greatly affected her life and how she felt about herself.

When looking at average self-esteem scores by age and week of intervention (1, 12 or 24), the following picture emerges (see Figure 4.7).

The graph shows that, for those aged 18–24, self-esteem peaked at the week 12 assessment; as it also did for males aged 25–40. There were slight reductions for males at week 24, but overall there was still an increase in self-esteem from week 1 to week 24. Of all age groups, males aged 18–24 had the highest self-esteem scores at week 1. The 25–40 age group for both males and females showed the highest increase in self-esteem by week 12 and the highest overall by week 24.

Females in all age groups had the lowest self-esteem scores at week 1 but then made significant gains. Females in the 25–40 and 41–54 age groups were the only ones showing an increase in self-esteem at week 24. A number of hypotheses can be made concerning these results: maybe a link exists between females in general being diagnosed later and thus experiencing specialist Enablement in a more positive way than others as a way to increase independence; maybe more mature people are emotionally more resilient and hence less anxious about specialist Enablement coming to an end; maybe more mature people are better at sustaining improvements in the skills they have learnt; or maybe females are more realistic about the goals of independence. Our sample of participants is too small to test these hypotheses but they may warrant further research.

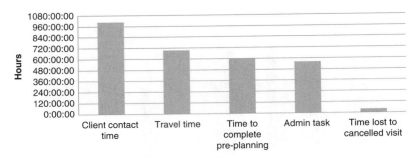

Figure 4.8 Overall analysis of staff time

Enablement resource analysis

The Enablement workers were occupational therapy assistants (OTAs), overseen by an occupational therapist. Each OTA was responsible for only four to five clients at any one time. Within the specialist Enablement intervention, workers spent their time on a number of activities (Figure 4.8), as described below.

Most OTA time was spent on client contact. However, as specialist Enablement is a high-quality, person-centred intervention, unsurprisingly a large amount of preparation is necessary, such as the creation of visual boards and laminated photographs. The amount of time spent on travelling reflects the fact that the ASC Team covers the whole of Kent. The amount of time lost to cancelled visits is relatively small and appears to indicate that the individuals valued the service and were motivated to engage.

Cost-setting analysis

Kent County Council uses a cost-setting tool to assess each individual's personal budget (the allocation of money that will be required to meet their assessed needs). This tool was applied following the needs assessment conducted by the case managers who recruited individuals for the research project. A case manager's calculation of the care and support an individual may need is a professional judgement that will ultimately be influenced by normative considerations – hence it is not scientific. The cost-setting tool was applied at weeks 1, 12 and 24. The Enablement team were not aware of participants' personal budgets.

In terms of average weekly cost over the Enablement period, Figure 4.9 shows reductions, and hence savings, for males and females in all age groups over the Enablement period.

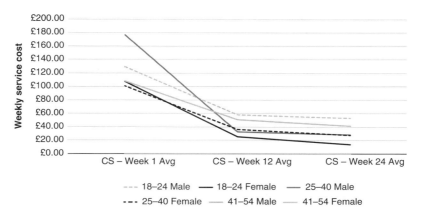

Figure 4.9 Average weekly service cost

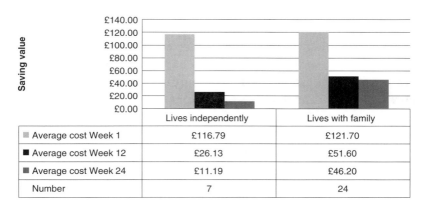

	Lives independently	Lives with family
▨ Average cost Week 1	£116.79	£121.70
▪ Average cost Week 12	£26.13	£51.60
▪ Average cost Week 24	£11.19	£46.20
Number	7	24

Figure 4.10 Reduction in service cost

A very slight decrease in cost was again noted at the point of longitudinal review, in all groups, at week 24. This may indicate that individuals may be able to sustain the skills they learnt during the specialist Enablement intervention. In terms of average savings, there was relatively little difference in cost-reduction between men and women.

Comparing the reduction in cost between individuals living independently and those living with their families, the following picture emerges (Figure 4.10).

A greater reduction in service costs for those who live independently is evident between weeks 1 and 24. Research participants who live with their family experienced the same pattern of cost-reduction but savings were not as substantial (it is acknowledged that this is the larger cohort). The results may relate to family dynamics; that is, family members may not recognise that Enablement participants are now more able and thus the level of care they supply can be reduced. Family members might also not realise that they may need to give a greater level of freedom to their adult child. This finding suggests that individuals who still live at home cannot be 'enabled' in isolation from their family.

According to the results of the 24-week reviews, post-Enablement costs continued to decline for both clients who live independently and those who live with their family.

Exploring the link between average savings and diagnosed co-morbidity produced the following findings (Figure 4.11).

Average savings are highest for those who also have a diagnosis of ADHD. Those with long-term mental health issues generated similar savings to participants with neither of these recognised conditions. This finding indicates that such issues did not have a negative impact on savings. During the specialist Enablement intervention there were, however, issues with individuals who had ADHD or mental health problems: in one case a female had untreated ADHD which affected provision, and in another case a male ended the intervention early because he exhibited significant mental health issues and was thus referred to mental health services.

When we add an extra dimension – gender – it can be seen that the two groups generating the largest cost-savings are males with ADHD

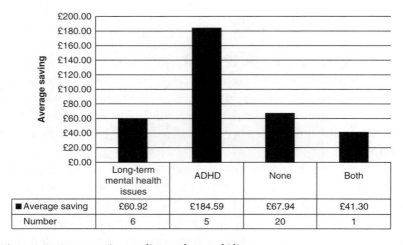

	Long-term mental health issues	ADHD	None	Both
■ Average saving	£60.92	£184.59	£67.94	£41.30
Number	6	5	20	1

Figure 4.11 Average saving per diagnosed co-morbidity

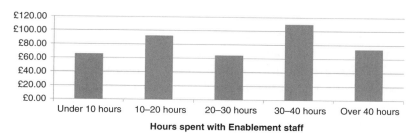

Figure 4.12 Average saving per actual contact time

and females with autism only. As Enablement is a highly specialist approach for those with autism, this may suggest that interventions of a neurodevelopmental nature would help anyone with autism and/or ADHD.

In terms of savings, the research project also wanted to assess the optimum level of intervention required to achieve the best cost outcome. Figure 4.12 shows cost savings by contact time, over the course of the complete 12-week intervention period.

The findings seem to indicate that cost avoidance was a positive factor within all levels of support. On the face of it, provision of 30+ hours over a 12-week period seemed to yield very good results. For some people, fewer hours produced satisfactory results. The Enablement team were thus led by the needs of the individual. Proving a possible hypothesis that the more hours of intervention, the greater the cost outcomes would require a larger sample of participants and deeper analysis of the number of participants in each Enablement cohort. It may also be significant that, for many individuals, specialist Enablement was their first experience of community-based support; that is, not provided by their family or school. For this reason, therefore, Enablement was not building upon previous specialist support.

Assessment of Motor Processing Skills

The Assessment of Motor Processing Skills (AMPS) is used to measure how well a person performs familiar activities of daily living (ADL). The AMPS can be used with any person, regardless of diagnosis or age, as long as they have a developmental age of at least two years and are familiar with performing some ADL tasks. The AMPS includes over 125 ADL tasks, from very easy self-care tasks to multi-step domestic tasks (including outdoor tasks and shopping). The AMPS has been standardised based on an international sample of over 196,000 people between the ages of 2 and 100+ years.

The occupational therapist administers the AMPS by observing a person perform two familiar and relevant ADL tasks in a natural, task-relevant environment. The therapist then scores the quality of 36 skills demonstrated by the individual during that task performance. The occupational therapist then uses AMPS software to generate a results report.

The AMPS measures represent how well the person performs ADL tasks in terms of physical effort, efficiency, safety and independence. These measures take into consideration the difficulty of the tasks the person performed and the unique scoring severity of the occupational therapist administering the AMPS. The occupational therapist can use a person's AMPS measures to plan occupation-based and occupation-focused intervention, develop occupation-focused goals and write occupation-focused documentation. AMPS results can also be used as outcome measures – providing evidence that a person's occupational performance has changed.

Evaluation of change

Evaluating change is quite a technical process but provides highly valued evidence about a person's ability. When the AMPS is used to evaluate change in a person's ADL ability, the person performs two standardised ADL tasks for each AMPS observation, the first at week 1, prior to the commencement of the Enablement support, and the second at week 12, when it finishes. ADL motor and ADL process ability measures are then compared using AMPS software, which determines whether the person's ADL ability has improved, stayed the same or declined. The software is also able to evaluate the meaningfulness of any change based on whether the change is great enough to be observable and whether it is likely to be statistically significant.

Observable change

Two ADL motor or two ADL process ability measures that differ by at least 0.3 logits (the AMPS units of change) in a practical and meaningful way indicate an observable change in ADL ability. A higher ADL motor or ADL process ability measure for the second AMPS observation indicates that there has been an observable improvement in the person's ADL ability. If two ADL motor or two ADL process ability measures do not differ by 0.3 logits, they can be considered to be essentially the same; there has been no observable change between week 1 and week 12.

Significant change

The person's standard error of measurement (SE) values for each of the AMPS measures can be used to determine whether the change between week 1 and week 12 is likely to be statistically significant. For example, if the change between week 1 and week 12 ADL motor ability measures is at least the sum of the SEs for each of those measures, the person's ADL motor ability has likely changed in a statistically meaningful way.

Figure 4.13 shows the outcomes of the evaluations of change after 12 weeks of Enablement intervention for the 22 people out of 30 who agreed to the measurement of their Motor and process skills. This graph shows that 20 people had made an observable improvement in their motor skills and 17 of these were statistically significant; 18 had made an observable improvement in their process skills and 16 of these

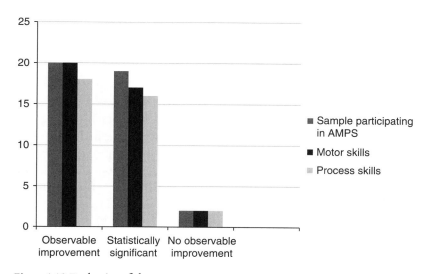

Figure 4.13 Evaluation of change

were statistically significant. Two people had made no improvement in either their motor or processing skills.

Occupational therapists commonly use ADL assessments as evidence to support decisions regarding a person's need for assistance if they are to live in the community. In support of this practice, the literature indicates that ADL ability is one of the strongest predictors of global functioning within the community. When using the results of an AMPS observation to predict a person's potential to live independently, the following guidelines can be applied:

> If the person's ADL motor ability is above 1.5 logits and their ADL process ability is above 1.0 logits, they are likely (86% chance) to live independently in the community. This profile is the strongest indicator of independence in the community.

> If the person's ADL motor ability is below 1.5 logits and their ADL process ability is below 1.0 logits, they are likely (83% chance) to need assistance to live in the community.

> If the person's ADL motor ability is below 1.0 logits and their ADL process ability is below 0.7 logits, they are likely to need assistance to live in the community and may even need moderate to maximal support.

The AMPS was specifically designed to measure ADL ability not community independence, thus the results of an AMPS observation should not be the sole criterion for predicting a person's need for assistance living in the community. The results of other assessments and professional reasoning will also be considered to accurately determine a person's need for assistance to live in the community.

Figure 4.14 shows initial AMPS observations at week 1 prior to the commencement of Enablement support. Seventeen people had motor ability scores above 1.5 logits and 14 people had processing ability scores above 1.0 logits. Three had motor ability scores below 1.5 logits and four had processing ability scores below 1.0 logits. Nobody had a motor ability score below 1.0 logits and two had a process ability score below 0.7 logits.

Figure 4.15 shows that 20 people had motor ability scores above 1.5 logits and 19 had process ability scores above 1.0, while 1 person had process ability scores below 1.0 logits. Nobody had a motor ability score below 1.0 logits or a process ability score below 0.7 logits.

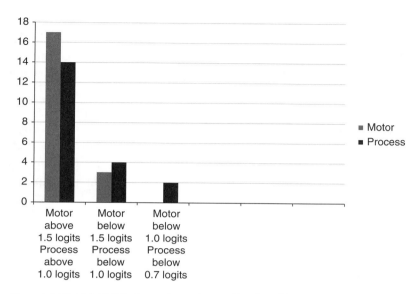

Figure 4.14 Initial AMPS observations prior to offer of Enablement support

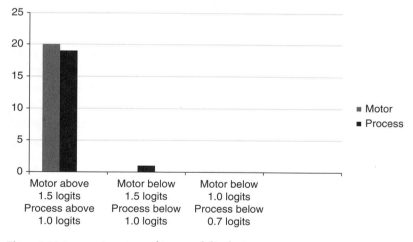

*Figure 4.15 Increase in motor and process ability logits
following 12 weeks of Enablement support*

In summary, this suggests that all 20 participants have benefitted from practising their chosen activities of daily living. What is more, according to the AMPS 86 per cent have a chance of living independently in the community. Some were recommended very small support packages to help them continue to develop their independent living skills. Figure 4.15 also suggests that with Enablement support the participants have been able to increase their processing abilities, which further suggests that understanding how individual autistic people learn is key. This helps validate our findings, in particular the use of visual materials.

The AMPS assessment, together with the sensory profile, really helped us to work within each client's own context and learning preferences. We looked at how participants process information best, that is, in visual or written form, or both, and their preferred learning style. We believe that the significant improvement in participants' processing abilities was partially attributable to their learning and understanding of new tasks in the context of their own home or community, using their own goods and equipment.

Vignettes

The testimonies in the vignettes and case studies are provided with the person's permission and are anonymised.

The client vignettes relate to life-changing personal outcomes. They concern Wendy, who was helped to self-manage and was able to transfer her increased functional ability to help her wider family, some of whom also had autism; John, who was supported in the workplace and stated that, following the Enablement intervention, he no longer had suicidal thoughts; and Abigail, who slept for the first time in many years and reduced her dependency upon her mother, who was herself increasingly unable to provide an adequate level of support for her daughter.

Wendy

Wendy had an ASC condition and children who were also on the autistic spectrum. Wendy had problems managing the home environment, which was very cluttered; this affected her caring for her children. Wendy wanted support to better manage her home environment. Her sensory profile indicated that she did not like touching or being touched and that she struggled with personal care. She was helped to improve her personal care using hand-over-hand assistance. With Wendy's consent, the occupational therapist put her hand over Wendy's to demonstrate how much pressure and movement was required to use her lady shaver effectively and safely.

Wendy was also helped to organise and plan her environment with the use of visual supports (her goal was to have a family meal sitting together at a table). Wendy's children also benefitted from the visual supports as these helped them see where things were to be kept and soon a visual timetable was established for the whole family. Wendy was helped to clean and clear her environment, with some support from her husband. The outcomes of the intervention involved the whole family. Wendy, with support from her family, managed her environment much better; everyone now shared meal times at the table; her children no longer needed support from other agencies; and Wendy did not require continuing support from the ASC Team.

John

John was struggling to cope with his job. He had diagnoses of ADHD and autism and did not feel that his peers and managers understood him. He had recently left his family home to live independently for the first time in his own flat. The occupational therapist assessed his interactions with others using the Assessment of Communication and Interaction Skills (ACIS) tool, observing him in a variety of environments: at work, going out for lunch with his colleagues and at home with his support worker. The ACIS identified areas that he could work on with the support worker alongside utilising the National Autistic Society SocialEyes programme – a social skills and social understanding package. With John's consent, the ACIS outcomes were shared with his managers and measures were introduced to address his problems interacting with others in the workplace, including regular daily meetings with his manager to discuss any problems, a flow chart to address queries and a work mentor sitting next to him to answer questions in the moment. The outcomes of the Enablement intervention were as follows: John found work much more manageable and indeed won an award for meeting his work-related targets. He began joining his peers for lunch and socialising with them. He told us that we had really helped him on an emotional level and to better understand his autism and ADHD. He no longer had suicidal thoughts. His ADHD medication was increased, which helped him to sustain focus at both work and home. John continued to have a small package of support for two hours a week to work through his emotions and help him to set up his new home. He continues to do well at work and now has his own family.

Abigail

Abigail is a young woman with an ASC who was highly dependent on her mother for support with washing, dressing and cooking. Abigail would not sleep without her mother beside her at night. A sensory profile assessment indicated the need for weighted therapy and she was provided with a weighted blanket. This helped her to sleep for the first time in years. Abigail learnt to cook independently and to see to her personal care. She was also helped to apply to college. The Enablement outcomes were: Abigail was assessed as needing fewer hours of support (at commencement of the intervention she required 30); she became more skilled in activities of everyday living, which reduced pressure on her carer; and she enrolled on a course at a local college. Abigail sustained her newly acquired skills at 24 weeks. She is continuing to do well at college and regularly posts pictures of her artwork for us to see. She is cooking meals for herself and her mother, and her personal assistant is continuing to promote her independence in activities of daily living and helping her to engage in her community.

Case studies

The three case studies below are more comprehensive accounts of personal outcomes achieved through the Enablement process. Each case study is headed by a photograph that is a self-defined symbolic reference to each individual's progress.

Jenny
Referral, data gathering and assessment

Jenny is a 30-year-old married woman with a young son. She is very reliant on her mother's daily support with household tasks. Jenny was referred to the ASC Team following a late diagnosis of autistic spectrum disorder in March 2015. Two years previously, as a result of the stress and anxiety she experienced in her professional role, Jenny had resigned from her job. She reported that she had often had meltdowns at the weekend and had not been eating and drinking properly. Jenny currently works three hours a week in an after-school club and provides full-time care for her son. Jenny already received support from the Kent Adult Sensory Team because she had severe auditory sensory difficulties resulting in extreme reactions to sound, tone and volume. This difficulty continued to impact greatly on her life and made her dependent on her mother. Jenny's autism diagnosis was accompanied by a recommendation that she be assessed by an occupational therapist. The report stated: 'She requires more strategies and support to help her manage at home and particularly as the demands and needs of her son change over time.' Jenny consented

Figure 4.16 Jenny's chicken tikka masala

and was subsequently referred by her social worker to the 12-week Enablement intervention to further identify her functional needs, strengths and limitations.

It was important to gather continuous data throughout Jenny's Enablement intervention. This was gained using various assessments and tools, including the Spectrum Star™, observation, listening and analysis, all of which contributed to evaluation of her progress and goal attainment.

The Spectrum Star™ helped Jenny see that her autism impacted upon her in the following domains and to these levels:

(*Note*: 9–10 = Choice and reliance; 7–8 = Learning for yourself; 5–6 = Stable; 3–4 = Accepting some support; 1–2 = Autism is a major barrier)

Physical health: 3.5

Living skills and self-care: 2.5

Well-being and self-esteem: 4

Sensory differences: 2

Communication: 5

Social skills: 3

Relationships: 7

Socially responsible behaviour: 8

Time and activities: 3

Whilst Jenny self-assessed the impact of her autism, there is also an impact, maybe less recognised by her, of her co-existing conditions, for example her diagnosed sensory condition.

Planning and preparation for intervention

It was important to use all the available information on Jenny to formulate an assessment of her functional abilities and needs to determine the goals to be achieved. Jenny's self-care, productivity and leisure issues were considered and Jenny was able to prioritise issues that were most important to her. Areas to develop had been identified through assessments such as the Assessment of Motor and Processing Skills and the completion of a sensory profile (Brown and Dunn 2002).

INITIAL DIFFICULTIES EXPERIENCED BY JENNY

- Problems cleaning her home independently.

- Inability to plan and structure time and/or organise environment in order to carry out tasks.

- Severe aversion to certain smells, particularly cleaning products containing bleach and disinfectant.

- Problems cooking the main meal for her family as a result of her inability to sequence tasks within a timeframe and her aversion to smells.

- Worrying that her young son is missing out on opportunities to engage with other children because she finds attending toddler groups difficult as a result of her issues with social communication and anxiety.

- Worrying about her reliance on her mother, who is visiting in the role of 'carer' rather than mother and grandmother.

Jenny was able to identify the following goals as the focus of her 12-week intervention:

- To have greater control over my environment and anxiety.

- To be able to plan and structure my time effectively around the needs of my family.

- To develop skills to allow me to manage my home with greater ease.

- To increase my confidence and overall well-being.

Implementing intervention

Jenny's identified goals were written in the form of an action plan setting out how they were going to be worked towards over the 12-week period with the assistance of her one-to-one Enablement support worker. The overall aim of this part of the Enablement support process was to help Jenny practise the skills she needed to achieve her individual outcomes. Jenny worked with the Enablement occupational therapist to devise an action plan of intervention and negotiate the time and duration of each of her visits. From the analysis of assessments and data collected from Jenny we were able to identify that her preferred learning style was pictorial. Jenny was encouraged to be involved in selecting appropriate pictorial resources and assisting her support worker to formulate an established routine from which to work. Jenny was able to provide feedback on her own progress and concerns. Jenny's Assessment of Motor and Process skills (AMPS; Fisher and Bray Jones 2010) identified the following areas of deficit that could be addressed throughout the Enablement process:

- Positioning of her body (motor skills)

- Obtaining and holding objects (motor skills)

- Organising the spacing of objects (process skills)

Jenny had chosen two AMPS tasks that would give her practice in planning and organising her time and activities, areas that she found particularly challenging:

- Putting away clean dishes from the dishwasher

- Giving the cat dry food and water

These two tasks were related to her overall goals of increasing her independence and confidence in managing her family and her environment. The planning and intervention involved showing Jenny how she could improve her skills through practice (acquisitional skills) – for example, she was able to practise her body position by modelling that of her support worker when emptying the dishwasher – and adaptive strategies, such as using noise-cancelling headphones to help her filter out unwanted sensory stimuli that were affecting her ability to maintain her focus on the task. This approach introduced her to alternative ways of doing things and the use of specialist equipment. Noise-cancelling headphones were trialled in line with the findings of her sensory profile. Jenny was unable to filter out background noises as a result of her severe sensory differences. This had a profound negative effect on her ability to carry out activities of daily living, as she often felt overwhelmed and overstimulated, which could lead to her experiencing high levels of anxiety and at times having a total 'meltdown'. Using noise-cancelling headphones that filtered out much of the noise which was distracting her meant that Jenny was able to focus on the task in hand. The headphones had another benefit for Jenny – they also filtered out some olfactory stimuli (smells).

According to Jenny:

The first time I went up to clean the bathroom I was sweating! I felt worried and sick. I was trying not to hold my breath as I was so anxious. My Enablement support worker explained that we were just going to clean the toilet and that would be a big first step. I was worried about the smell of the bleach – I hate the smell of bleach. I find it suffocating and usually my mum has to clean my bathroom while I hide somewhere with something wrapped around my face. My support worker showed me how the headphones worked and, although I could hear her, I couldn't hear anything else. I felt a bit silly wearing headphones to clean a toilet and I was sure that this was going to be a complete waste of time but she reassured me and talked me through each stage.

A very strange thing happened. I couldn't smell the bleach like before – I could smell bleach but it wasn't making me want to run or be nervous. I did wonder if I had bought a different brand of bleach but they explained that using the headphones had helped with my sensory overload. I was still very sweaty but I didn't feel as many of the physical symptoms as I had before. By the third week I was cleaning the entire bathroom. In fact, I was cleaning the entire house. The Enablement support worker and I picked a spot in each room

Figure 4.17 Jenny's toolboxes

> *where I always started and I had a list of tasks that was specific to each room. We also made some 'toolboxes' to keep under the sink with the sprays and cloths that I needed for each job. We devised the timetable so that a room got done at the same time each week.*

Jenny was given assistance to arrange a number of self-help aids such as the cleaning toolboxes shown in Figure 4.17. Jenny was also helped to organise her environment through the use of prompts on a visual routine board. This allowed Jenny to structure her day and everything she wanted to achieve within it.

As Jenny reports:

> *We made a board on which I could build a daily timetable. I hadn't realised how unstructured my days were and how anxious this was making me feel. This was something my son absolutely loved as he knew what each of the pictures meant (and he knew the train picture meant time to play!). I found myself knowing that I had to put the washing on in the morning so that I could dry it on the line by the end of the day. I had a card to show which room to clean on that day so I could plan that in too. It also reminded me of the need to take frequent breaks, feed my pets and take care of myself.*

Jenny was keen to cook for her family and, for this, required pictorial sequence recipes so that she could follow them, plus support to recognise what equipment and materials she would need. Recipes were adapted to meet Jenny's requirements and she was encouraged to practise the task.

Jenny states:

> *I found some recipes that I wanted to cook and first we made some simple biscuits. The recipe had always looked appealing but the text was in big blocks rather than step-by-step instructions. There was also very little information about what equipment to get and what ingredients. The Enablement support worker and I went through everything slowly and we got everything ready before we started. She then talked me through each stage and gave me tips. The following week we decided to try making a chicken tikka masala. It seemed so complicated, with lots of ingredients. The Enablement support worker had prepared the same recipe in a different format so that it had different sections for equipment, ingredients and the method. Using the headphones, and with a bit of help, I made the meal. I don't think I have ever seen my husband eat anything so fast. There was also enough for another meal later in the week, which really helped on a day when I was busier.*

Jenny also experienced poor sleep patterns, reporting that she often struggled to get to sleep because she felt highly alert prior to going to bed. Jenny was provided with a massage mattress, which helped her focus on relaxation, which in turn regulated her senses so that she was able to feel less alert prior to bedtime.

Evaluating outcomes

It was important to measure and evaluate Jenny's Enablement interventions in relation to her agreed goals. This was achieved by evaluating her performance through observations, Jenny's feedback and specific assessments such as AMPS. (Additional outcomes were also recorded and evaluated within the wider ASC Team. These included Jenny's evaluations of her Spectrum Star™ and self-esteem questionnaire.)

Jenny was initially assessed using AMPS. Following 12 weeks of intervention, including practising the deficit areas identified within the AMPS assessment, Jenny was re-assessed, again using the AMPS, to evaluate her progress. Her results showed an observable increase in her activities of daily living, in both her motor and processing ability, and that this increase was likely to be statistically significant.

In relation to her progress, Jenny states:

I have gone from having my mum and husband do everything around the house to doing nearly everything by myself using the resources and skills I have been given. I can now clean all the rooms in the house. We have cut food bills and food waste as I can plan what I want to eat and understand how to check what I already have and what I need to buy. People are really starting to notice. Family say I'm more confident and say better things about myself because I am proud of what I have managed to do. My mum isn't coming over to spend three hours cleaning so we are having time to talk and play with my son. My husband has noticed that my anxiety levels have dropped slightly and he cannot believe how much I have learnt in such a short time. My son and I have a better bond because I feel less guilty about not managing everything and I'm more relaxed and organised. He also asks for the chicken curry and cake almost constantly.

I have won a competition to write a blog for the Hairy Bikers *diet club and they've given me hundreds of recipes to try. I want to work on some of these so I can show other autistic people that it's possible, with some adaptations, to be able to make some really nice food. This will mean I have lots of recipes to choose from to make meals well into the future as well. I would never have dreamed of doing this just a few months ago.*

I really feel that I learnt a lot in the time I spent with the Enablement team. I am a little anxious about the longer-term sustaining of the skills.

The whole experience so far has been so positive and I would recommend it as a very valuable and constructive experience.

As a reminder, these were the goals that Jenny set out to achieve:

- To have greater control over my environment and anxiety.

- To be able to plan and structure my time effectively around the needs of my family.

- To develop skills to allow me to manage my home with greater ease.

- To increase my confidence and overall well-being.

Jenny achieved all of her goals, although she still wanted to improve her social skills and increase her confidence in the wider community. Her Spectrum Star™ reflected these outcomes. Jenny had gained a greater understanding of her sensory needs and now had strategies she could draw upon to enable her to live and explore the life she wanted.

Cooking a chicken tikka masala enabled her to ascribe meaning to her roles as wife and mother, increased her confidence and self-esteem and allowed her to learn new skills. It is not surprising that Jenny chose her chicken curry photograph to represent the symbolic value of the Enablement experience.

Jenny's Spectrum Star™ review at the end of the Enablement period (12 weeks) demonstrated a positive change in all but one area (social skills), which Jenny was still seeking to address. Scores in bold indicate the positive changes:

Physical health: 3.5 **(8)**

Living skills and self-care: 2.5 **(7)**

Well-being and self-esteem: 4 **(5)**

Sensory differences: 2 **(4)**

Communication: 5 **(5)**

Social skills: 3 **(2)**

Relationships: 7 **(8)**

Socially responsible behaviour: 8 **(9)**

Time and activities: 3 **(5)**

Results from Jenny's initial self-esteem questionnaire indicated that her emotional well-being and self-esteem were very low – she had given herself a score of 7. Following the Enablement intervention, she gave herself a score of 18, a significant improvement.

Jenny's original indicative/estimated personal budget was to cover six hours a week. At the end of Enablement, Jenny was assessed as needing only two hours of support a week because she wanted to continue to build on her success with only a small amount of ongoing support.

Dominic

Referral, data gathering and analysis

Dominic had been referred to the ASC Team by a clinical psychologist. It was felt that a social care assessment was needed following his recent

Figure 4.18 Dominic's dog

ASD diagnosis. Dominic also had a long-term diagnosis of attention deficit disorder (ADD) and depression. He was living with his parents and sister, all of whom worked while he remained home alone for many hours with only his dog (Holly) for company. Dominic was reliant on his family for many activities of daily living, including the cooking of his food. He had poor sleep patterns that impacted on his ability to keep appointments and establish daily routines. Dominic was introduced to the specialist Enablement team. The occupational therapist gave him information about the benefits of a holistic occupational therapy approach and how it could help him, and stressed that the intervention would be client-centred. Using the Spectrum Star™ and information from the psychologist, Dominic came to understand the reasons for his referral and consented to partake in the specialist Enablement intervention.

Planning and preparing for intervention

We initially used the Spectrum Star™ with Dominic (during a semi-structured interview), followed by other occupational therapy tools and assessments (interest and role checklists, sensory profile and

AMPS). We also listened to Dominic and gave him information about his diagnoses (ASD and ADD). This approach enabled us to explore his occupational performance in all areas. Consideration was given to the three occupational therapy domains (self-care, productivity and leisure) and Dominic and the occupational therapist were able to identify and document the most important priorities for him (that is, goals to be achieved). These were:

- To be able to travel on a bus to a chosen location independently.

- To be more confident about making snacks to ensure he eats regularly.

- To be able to access the local gym as a regular activity.

- To establish a weekly routine structured around managing time and activities/appointments.

- To feel confident taking the dog out for a walk.

Dominic's limiations were:

- A long history of depression, which impacted his abilities, mood and levels of motivation.

- Sleeping difficulties, which impact his ability to establish routines and activities during the day.

- A diagnosis of ADD. Although this difficulty was identified at school, Dominic has never been seen for follow-up or received support. This disorder is having a huge impact on his life, particularly related to his inability to keep to task and racing thoughts that affect his focus and sleep patterns.

- Sensory differences.

- Skill areas needing further practice, as identified by the AMPS assessment:

    - Obtaining and holding objects (motor skills)

    - Sustaining performance (motor skills)

    - Moving self and objects (motor skills)

    - Temporal organisation (process skills).

After observing Dominic complete some activities of daily living in his home, the occupational therapist discussed her findings with Dominic. He reported that he had been reliant on his family to prepare and cook his meals and that he often felt exhausted as a result of his poor sleep patterns, which then impacted on his ability to remember to take his medication. This helped Dominic to make sense of his symptoms and to determine the goals he wanted to achieve during the 12-week Enablement intervention.

Implementing intervention

Dominic's intervention was conducted both at home and in the community, on a one-to-one basis. Dominic worked with the Enablement occupational therapist to devise an action plan and to negotiate the time and duration of each of her visits. Dominic worked in partnership with the occupational therapist regarding any changes to this plan, and was encouraged throughout to discuss his views and concerns and to suggest alternative options, particularly on occasions when he struggled to leave the house.

The following approaches were used with Dominic:

- *Acquisitional* (through graded practice) – Dominic was helped to access the community using his dog as both a motivator and an asset. Holly provided a purpose for leaving the house and her walks were gradually extended as Dominic grew in confidence and was better able to recognise where he was. Dominic was keen to use public transport and was thus provided with a bus pass with companion – a local transport initiative for people with disabilities and their carers. Dominic was accompanied to his destination during the intervention period until, eventually, he was able to travel alone and meet his support worker only at his final destination. Regarding eating regularly, Dominic was encouraged to use a routine board and prompts to help him practise preparing and making his own snacks.

- *Compensatory* (through pictorial prompts and cues) – Dominic benefitted from the use of a visual timetable to establish a daily routine for both him and Holly. (The roles checklist had identified his dog as an important aspect of his life.) Dominic's sensory profile had identified that he might benefit from weighted therapy, thus he was encouraged to use a weighted blanket and Squease jacket. A Squease jacket is an inflatable deep pressure garment that, when inflated, applies a firm hug-like pressure to the person's upper body that can have a calming effect on them. It can be helpful to people who find it difficult to process and integrate sensory information from their body and their surroundings; for example, people who find it difficult to tell the difference between presenting sensory stimuli in the foreground and stimuli in the background and, as a consequence, receive all sensory information at the same time thus making everyday situations overwhelming and all the more stressful.

- *Asset-based* (using Dominic's dog and community resources) – Dominic had a keen interest in joining a gym and one was actually located within walking distance of his home. Dominic's GP was supportive regarding referring him for a specialist assessment so that he could access advice about how to better manage it; she also monitored his ongoing depression and medication for such.

Evaluating outcomes

While making steady progress, Dominic agreed that some of his limitations were still heavily impacting on his functional performance – namely, his ADD and depression. His sensory profile indicated the need for a weighted blanket and Squease jacket; a successful trial of the blanket resulted in Dominic establishing a better sleeping pattern. Dominic reported that:

The weighted blanket seems to have calmed everything down in my head. I feel more able to focus on getting to sleep.

Using his Squease jacket while out and about, he continued,

Gives me a feeling of confidence and reduces my anxieties to manageable levels so that I'm able to leave the house.

Dominic also had a visual routine board in place, which was clearly working well because he now had some structure to his day. Dominic had started to take an interest in making his own snacks as part of his routine, but agreed that he would need continued support in cooking main meals.

Dominic was re-assessed at week 12 using the AMPS to evaluate the progress he had made during the Enablement intervention. His results revealed an observable increase in both his motor and process abilities related to activities of daily living, and it was likely that these increases were statistically significant.

Dominic was helped to visit his GP and discuss his ADD (he had not been given any support since his diagnosis as a young child) and subsequently his GP referred him for a specialist assessment in this area. Dominic's mood and motivational levels were also a cause for concern so he agreed to be referred to the local mental health team for further support. We were able to use Dominic's dog as a resource to encourage him to leave the house using a graded approach. 'Grading' is a process whereby occupational therapists view an activity on a continuum from simple to complex and introduce elements of it gradually so as not to overwhelm the individual. For example, Dominic was helped to walk to the end of his road as the initial part of the route until he was confident in doing so independently; the next part of the route was then introduced. Learning his desired new route enabled him to access the wider community as part of his travel training. We also used his responsibility for his dog as a means of establishing meaningful routines (Holly also seemed to benefit from the Enablement intervention and became much less anxious too). Dominic was also interested in using a local gym but had never got round to it, he stated in his initial assessment. At the end of the Enablement period Dominic was attending this gym as part of his weekly routine and was able to acknowledge the positive effect this was having on his mood. While Dominic achieved his goals, he still required ongoing assistance in the form of a small support package to continue to work on his wider goals for independent living.

Jacob

Referral, data gathering and analysis

Jacob was referred to the ASC Team by his mother, who reported that he had been diagnosed with an ASD at the age of four. Jacob had been

Figure 4.19 Jacob's reindeer

known to Children and Family Services as a child as a result of his autism and co-existing mental health condition (he is bipolar), which at times severely impacted both himself and his family. Jacob takes medication to help manage his conditions; however, he reports that it contributes to his weight gain. Jacob was home tutored by his mother to GCSE level, then attended a college of further education where he gained additional qualifications in information technology and horticulture. Since leaving college Jacob has completed some retail work experience. Jacob has recently moved to his own privately rented one-bedroom flat in the same building as his mother; she continues to support him with prompts to attend to his personal care, and with activities of daily living such as cooking, cleaning and budgeting. Jacob struggled to use public transport; however, he enjoyed socialising with his friends, who he invited to his flat every other week to play on his Xbox and watch football. Jacob additionally struggled with his sleep patterns and generally slept from 3–6 a.m. Jacob's mother was concerned that Jacob still required support to establish the daily routines that would enhance his independence at home, and was keen that he be offered opportunities which could lead to potential employment. Jacob was introduced to the specialist Enablement team and consented to explore means of achieving his goals.

Planning and preparing for intervention

Initially, the Spectrum Star™ was used with Jacob in the form of a semi-structured interview, together with other occupational therapy tools and assessments (interest and role checklists, sensory profile and AMPS) to elicit areas of priority for Jacob and to help the occupational therapist understand his level of functioning across all areas of his life (self-care, productivity and leisure). These tools and assessments helped the occupational therapist and Jacob to identify and document his most important priorities (goals to be achieved); these were:

- To be confident in cooking healthy main meals.

- To clean and maintain his flat independently.

- To find work experience.

Jacob's limitations are:

- At times he does not take his medication, which impacts on his ability to focus and his overall mental health.

- He can depend on his mother for both physical and psychological support on a regular basis, which impacts on their relationship.

Implementing intervention

Jacob's intervention was to be carried out both at home and in the community, on a one-to-one basis. Jacob worked with the Enablement occupational therapist to devise an action plan for intervention and negotiate the time and duration of each of her visits. He set out his goals and together they established how to work towards them over the following 12 weeks. Jacob worked in partnership to agree any changes to his plan and was encouraged throughout to provide feedback on his progress and to suggest alternative options, particularly when he struggled to get up in the morning and on days when he did not want to take his medication.

The following approaches were used with Jacob:

- *Acquisitional* (through graded practice) – This covered travel training involving being able to identify the correct bus stop, read the timetable, access the bus, purchase a ticket, identify ultimate destination and alight at correct stop consistently and safely. Cooking tasks involved planning of healthy snacks and meals, shopping and budgeting, storing things correctly, using new appliances, operating controls and cooking chosen meals.

- *Compensatory* (through visuals, pictorial-sequenced prompts and cues) – This involved establishing a daily routine and using a calendar, visual sequenced recipes, a dosset box for medication and alarms on his mobile phone. Jacob was keen to be supported using this approach, although reluctant to have too much visual information around his home (on show) as he was keen to be seen by his peers as managing his life and environment. Coupled with the acquisitional approaches, Jacob was happy to store his personalised cooking recipes in a folder that he could access when needed.

- *Asset-based* (Jacobs's mother and wider community resources) – Jacob's mother was keen for him to learn for himself and provided opportunities for him to work out the controls on the shared washing machine. She also helped Jacob to budget and pay his bills. Jacob's mother had also found a voluntary job in the horticultural field and arranged for him to attend an interview; this provided an ideal opportunity for him to work on the skills he needed to prepare for and get to work.

Evaluating outcomes

Jacob was helped to establish routines in his flat and to manage tasks independently. He was able to discuss strategies that he was willing to explore and implement to support the learning of new skills (such as making more use of the alarm on his mobile phone to prompt him to do tasks within a certain timeframe). Jacob was helped to prepare for and attend his interview (which was the focus of his travel training) and was delighted by his success in securing a position as a volunteer. Jacob's new volunteer role became the focus of his Enablement work as it required him to follow a structured daily routine throughout the working week. Jacob learnt to use his weekly routine planner (initially in the form of a calendar and later a white board placed above the area where he made himself tea in the mornings) to better organise his time and activities. Jacob was assessed at work by the occupational therapist and strategies were provided to support him in the workplace. Jacob was able to travel independently and safely to his workplace. Two weeks into his volunteer role, Jacob did not take his medication, which resulted in him getting up late and missing his bus for work. One of his responsibilities at work was to open the gates for other members of the team and obviously there was a problem that day. Jacob reported that this incident made him realise that others relied on him and the necessity of taking his medication. He attended work on time thereafter. Jacob liked to keep his flat looking nice and took pride in cleaning it with the support of a cleaning schedule. At times Jacob reported that he was struggling to strike a balance between entertaining his friends and going to bed early. He was helped to manage this issue using his visual calendar and work schedule, which showed him when he would be free to see his friends. Jacob was keen to prioritise his volunteer work and noted that, as none of his friends had jobs, it was up to him to organise get-togethers at appropriate times for him. Jacob benefitted from following a structured routine that enabled him to understand what he needed to do each day.

Jacob reported that, while he continued to see his friends, he still struggled with managing his mental health needs; he was duly referred to the community mental health team. During this period of difficulty with his mental health, he nevertheless stated:

> I am so proud that I have been offered this opportunity to be a volunteer and work with people who need my support as I like supporting other people who are more challenged than me.

Jacob's photograph shows some of the reindeers he and other service users made at a fund-raising event at work. He has since been in touch to tell us:

> I have been offered a permanent position as a supervisor. I am enjoying being part of a team in which I can support others to achieve.

Jacob has been able to sustain his employment and continues to enjoy growing produce and making various item for sale. Most of all he is proud of what he has achieved and wants to share his success story with others.

In this chapter we presented the research results for all assessment measurements used by the Kent ASC Enablement intervention. We used a number of personal testimonies to bring the Enablement approach to 'life'. In the next, and final, chapter, we consider if we have met our research objectives, reflect on what we have learnt and discuss how Enablement provision could be improved in the future.

Bibliography

Brown, C. and Dunn, W. (2002) *Adolescent/Adult Sensory Profile*. San Antonio, TX: PsychCorp.

Burns, S. and MacKeith, J. (2012) *Spectrum Star*™. Triangle Consulting Social Enterprise Ltd. Accessed on 06/08/2017 at www.outcomestar.org.uk.

Fisher, A. and Bray Jones, K. (2010) *Assessment of Motor and Process Skills*. Volume 1: *Development, Standardization, and Administration Manual*, 7th edition. Fort Collins, CO: Three Star Press.

Mills, R. and Kenyon, S. (2013) 'Study in Pink: Prevalence study of females with autism in the four participating countries.' Accessed on 11/05/2017 at http://autisminpink. net.

Rosenberg, M. (1965) *Society and the Adolescent Self-image*. Princeton, NJ: Princeton University Press.

Chapter 5

Key Learning and Recommendations

Matt Bushell, Sandra Gasson and Ute Vann

In this chapter we seek to explore in more detail what we have learnt from the ASC specialist Enablement intervention, discussing further our key learning from the project and making recommendations where appropriate for improvement or development of the approach. We start by assessing briefly how far we have progressed towards our stated Enablement research objectives. We use the word *progress* deliberately because our Enablement analysis has not ended; we continue to provide Enablement to our clients and continue to evaluate measurements.

It is fair to say that the ASC specialist Enablement (social care research) intervention has exceeded our expectations thus far. First and foremost, the Enablement results to date demonstrate a great deal about the fortitude of the clients we are charged to support; a marginalised group whose needs are not universally understood and to whom support is rarely provided at a specialist level – particularly in adulthood and particularly towards people stated to be 'higher functioning'.

This was a very small-scale project, admittedly, but the qualitative results pose, we believe, great potential for the development of Enablement interventions within dedicated autism teams. We also hope that we have furthered the case made by the National Audit Office (2009) that autism teams are 'cost-effective'. This important point – critical to any debate regarding increasing autism teams globally – is explored, amongst other issues, in the section below.

Research objectives and results

The research project concerned the provision of a specialist Enablement intervention that used a functional, adaptive and sensory approach. The research was aimed at exploring the benefits, or lack thereof, of specialist Enablement for people with high-functioning autism or Asperger syndrome and whether it should be an integral part of support provision for adults on the autistic spectrum. The main question the research sought to answer was whether specialist Enablement intervention, with its use of occupational therapy tools and approaches, can facilitate positive change for the individual with high-functioning autism living in the community. Positive change was determined by whether the individual improved in the functional areas they themselves had indentified.

From a local authority perspective, the main question concerned achieving improved outcomes in the most cost-effective way: would specialist Enablement result in clients improving self-management so that they thus required fewer high-cost support packages?

Thirty participants completed the specialist Enablement intervention, of whom 23 were assessed 12 weeks post-completion to measure whether any improvement had been sustained. We believe that the research results demonstrate that, for the 30 people who completed the specialist Enablement intervention, its key objectives were met: specialist Enablement can facilitate positive change in terms of the self-management of high-functioning autistic people living in the community and can be cost-effective. For the 23 people who were also assessed 12 weeks after completion of the intervention, beneficial effects appear to have been sustained.

Looking at the different measurement tools used during the research, the self-assessed qualitative measurements proved most useful for illustrating the benefits of personalised specialist Enablement. The *Spectrum Star*^{TM} (Burns and MacKeith 2012) evidenced progression through the 'journey of change' for each participant, based on how they rated themselves in the different areas of functioning. The *participant exit questionnaire* focused on the *lived* experience of the participant and provided valuable feedback regarding what goals were set and achieved by the individuals and what longer-term benefits of the intervention individuals valued most.

The *carers' questionnaire* proved less valuable and was not fit for the purpose of measuring change in carers' time spent caring or caring responsibilities. Nevertheless, it provided some useful information, especially about potential gaps in support for carers.

The *self-esteem questionnaire* provided results that were encouraging but was also the measurement most affected by exterior forces/events and life events and anxieties. These phenomena could change how individuals feel throughout the day and make it difficult for autistic people to evaluate what happened over time. Results thus need to be treated with caution.

Cost-setting analyses evidenced reductions in estimated cost/personal budgets for all client types.

Key findings

Looking at the research results, the findings can be summed up as follows:

1. Spectrum Star™ mean averages show that, for all participants, the highest area of improvement at 12 and 24 weeks was in 'Living skills and self-care'. This is explained by the fact that most participants chose to work on learning new skills in those areas. The score for this area at 24 weeks appears to indicate that, for 23 participants measured at this stage, improvement was sustained. At 24 weeks, another area of high improvement was 'Sensory skills', which may indicate that advanced sensory work as an integral part of Enablement has sustaining potential. The older age group (those aged over 25 as opposed to 18–24) seemed to benefit most from the intervention. Participants identified their areas of most significant need as 'Well-being and self-esteem', 'Social skills' and 'Time and activities'; by weeks 12 and 24 some change had occurred. 'Relationships' and 'Communication' showed the smallest improvement – but an improvement overall between week 1 and week 24.

2. The participant exit questionnaire showed that the majority of participants set goals around activities of everyday living that were important to them. Achieving new skills such as independent travel, cooking and managing routines were valued most. When asked about the longer-term benefits of the specialist Enablement intervention, a high percentage of participants cited learning and sustaining new skills. Figure 4.7

shows that, for those aged 18–24, self-esteem peaked at the week 12 assessment; as it also did for males aged 25–40. There were slight reductions for males at week 24 but, overall, there was still an increase in self-esteem from week 1 to week 24. In terms of all age groups, males aged 18–24 had the highest self-esteem scores at week 1. In general, the 25–40 age group for both males and females showed the highest increase in self-esteem by week 12 and the highest overall by week 24.

3. The self-esteem questionnaire showed that males aged 18–24 had the highest self-esteem scores at week 1. In general, the 25–40 age group for both males and females showed the highest increase in self-esteem by week 12 and the highest overall by week 24. Females in all age groups had the lowest self-esteem scores at week 1 but then made significant gains. Females in the 25–40 and 41–54 age groups were the only ones showing an increase in self-esteem at week 24. As stated before, these results need to be treated with caution.

4. Seventeen people responded to the carers' questionnaire; most were female and aged 41–60. More than half had health problems of their own, and most estimated that they provided more than 20 hours of support per week. A high majority said that they had no practical support in their caring role.

5. In terms of finance and resources, specialist Enablement was evidenced to be cost-effective – both in terms of costs justifying the expenditure of hosting the service and costs justifying the outcomes. We hope that we proved the case for the latter in Chapter 4, but have said little thus far about *the costs justifying the expenditure*. To answer that here: during the Enablement research year – when deducting the cost of hosting the Enablement service (3 workers and some equipment) from the savings made on reduced care and support packages (over the 30 participants who completed all research measurements) – the provision paid for itself with an additional £60,000 over the year saved (avoided) in package costs. Cost-setting analysis overall evidenced a reduction in estimated cost/personal budgets for all client categories. There was little difference between males and females but data shows that there is a

greater reduction in cost for those who live independently than for those living with family. Cost continued to reduce to week 24. The cost analysis also indicated that participants with autism and co-existing ADHD displayed exceptional cost reductions. In comparison, participants with autism and a co-existing diagnosed mental health condition displayed less significant cost savings. Cost analysis of the average saving per actual contact time with staff demonstrated a saving in each range of hours provided; overall, it appeared that the more hours provided the greater the cost savings, but such a hypothesis would need to be tested for a much larger sample of Enablement participants.

Key learning and recommendations

The research results also posed some key learning points for us that we felt would be worthy of exploring further.

Using the Enablement framework as a key foundation for intervention

The specialist Enablement intervention was pivotal to the success of the intervention and, ultimately, positive change in research participants' lives. Occupational therapy conceptual frameworks (models) originate from theories, other models and evidence-based practice. They provide a way of thinking about how complex issues interact. They serve as a guideline for dealing with complexities by providing a framework to:

- Define the scope and boundaries of a profession.

- Describe its fundamental principles and values.

- Guide assessments, interventions and evaluation practices (Duncan 2006).

In Chapter 3 the pyramid of learning was introduced. Initially described by Ayres (1979), we have used it to demonstrate the need for a *bottom-up* approach when supporting autistic adults to achieve higher-level skills, such as those necessary for independent living.

Our pyramid of learning has evolved in our Enablement practice, and is based on that of Williams and Shellenberger (1996). Though our Enablement intervention focuses on functional skills and their sensory base, the pyramid clearly indicates strong links to theories of psycho-social development and fits well with Erikson's (1950) theory (described in Newman and Newman 2015), which looks at personality and the development of the ego identity. Although he does not address the sensori-motor influences, his work nonetheless remains the highest regarded and most affiliated to the levels that we clearly see in some adults with autism. Newman and Newman (2015) expand on Erikson's theory and highlight some key points:

- Our personality develops in stages and constantly changes as a result of exposure to new experiences and information gained from our daily interactions with others.

- Our social experiences have an impact on us throughout our lifespan.

- Our sense of self (ego identity) develops through our social interactions.

- Our sense of competence motivates our behaviours and actions.

- Each stage relates to becoming competent in one area of life, which can lead to a sense of mastery or a sense of failure if not managed well.

- At each stage, conflict is experienced that serves as a turning point in development, which can lead to developing a quality or failing to develop a quality, which further leads to potential for personal growth or potential for failure.

The pyramid of learning highlights how we develop as individuals and serves to justify the need for a clearly structured approach to gathering specific information. This framework has enabled us to understand the unique needs of each autistic person and their pathway for intervention. It has assisted us in understanding the type of difficulties that exist and why, and to identify which particular impacts of autism might have held an individual back from achieving success in previous interventions (often because the lower levels of the pyramid have not been identified or fully addressed). It highlights the need for a multidisciplinary team, in particular a psychologist working in amongst the other professionals.

Mucklow (2009) related the pyramid of learning to practical real-life experiences and used the metaphor of a house to demonstrate the bottom-up approach to helping young people understand their sensory system and what they can do to help themselves. We have found this metaphor useful as most of the adults we work with prefer materials to be presented in a visual way to help them process information. We have thus designed our own visual representation (see Figure 5.1) to not only represent our interventions but also help us identify gaps within our service and to translate these to a business case to demonstrate what we need as a service to support the wider needs of autistic adults.

First, to support adults with autism we need to understand how people develop as individuals and how those with autism are affected by their condition.

The *nurturing environment* is one in which an individual feels safe and has trusting relationships. 'Trust versus mistrust' is the first of Erikson's (1950) psychosocial stages and, according to him, is the most foundational and fundamental because trust is reliant on the dependability and quality of an individual's carers and on feeling safe and secure in the world. Erikson states that if an individual's care is inconsistent, or emotionally not available or rejecting, feelings of fear

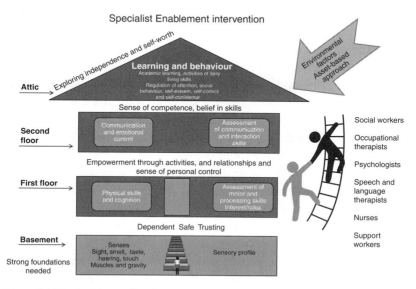

Figure 5.1 The Enablement foundation
Source: Sandra Gasson, based on the theoretical frameworks of Ayres (1979), Mucklow (2009), Erikson (1950) and Williams and Shellenberger (1996).

and mistrust will develop and the world will likely appear inconsistent and unpredictable to them.

Gaining the trust of some autistic adults can be difficult; however, it is a vital stage to be achieved prior to any intervention. Occupational therapists will gather much of their information from the person, their families and those who have been supporting them at this point. They may additionally draw on occupational therapy tools such as interest checklists to ascertain/elicit a person's interests and the value they place on such activities. It is often through a person's interests that we can start to build rapport.

We know that as a result of sensory processing differences many autistic adults experience the world differently. Addressing these needs is paramount to gaining an understanding of how they experience their world. Strong foundations in this area are necessary in order to achieve higher functioning skills. For example, if a person is struggling to filter out the sensory information they are constantly exposed to, it will impact on their ability to focus and directly affect successful interaction with their environment. Ultimately, until this is addressed further development will be impeded. Only when they are aware and helped to manage their sensory differences will they feel safe and be ready to develop their skills further. Thus, addressing sensory differences often is key to helping autistic people engage in learning and develop new skills.

Some autistic adults have an additional diagnosis of dyspraxia, which may impact their ability to undertake activities/tasks that require organising the body in such a way as to adapt and adjust to a number of steps. These activities/tasks often require a great deal of practice before they are mastered (but ultimately lead to a sense of empowerment and personal control). Activities at this level generally involve the ability to sequence a task and to make a mental plan of the necessary steps – or having an idea of how to do that task beforehand. Many individuals need lots of regular practice to master new skills, which can be difficult when they live with their family who provide a great deal of hands-on support and for whom provision of care is part of their daily routine.

Spatial awareness is an issue and we thus work with the individual to help them be more aware of where their body is in relation to others and objects. This awareness is necessary so that the individual can undertake activities safely; it is also applicable to understanding social distance – that is, proximity to others in different situations.

Another limitation is bilateral sequencing, which involves tasks such as cutting (often in the kitchen). Many autistic adults find certain sensory situations overwhelming; however, they will need to be able to attend to stimuli pertinent to the situation or task in hand and also screen out that which is irrelevant. They may need to be provided with strategies or equipment to help them reduce or eliminate overwhelming stimuli to give them the greatest opportunity to overcome these difficulties.

Some autistic adults have auditory processing difficulties. This is often the case for those who struggle to pay attention to and remember sequences of information presented orally and in particular when accompanied by other, distracting, stimuli. They may have difficulties in carrying out multi-step instructions and require more time to process information. Often these individuals will prefer to learn new tasks visually rather than being verbally advised what to do. Maximising opportunities for the individual to learn is critical. For the individual learning to cook, it may be necessary to create personalised visual sequenced steps in order for them to follow a recipe. Another approach is to provide photographs of their actual kitchen appliances, in order to help them understand how to operate the microwave or cooker, for example. Others may be able to follow more generalised pictorial prompts.

Maximising opportunities for engagement in meaningful activities is important for individuals; taking their interests into account can further enhance their ability to engage and broaden their attention. For example, they may spend hours playing computer games or watching films in their bedroom (solitary activities) but may be encouraged to attend a social group with others with the same interest to maximise opportunities to enhance their social interaction skills. Our peer support group provider in Kent decided to run computer gaming groups as a means of enabling young people who share this interest to also socialise in the process.

It is not uncommon for autistic adults and their families to discuss difficulties performing all activities of daily living. Our visual representation of a house (Figure 5.1) is particularly useful here because it enables occupational therapists to guide the individual (and their family) to look at other areas that may be impacting on their ability to perform these activities and their ability to move on with their life. We have also found gaps in our wider service, such as the need for a multidisciplinary team comprising psychologists, occupational therapists, speech and language therapists and specialist nurses to address the mental health, communication difficulties and other (emotional, sexual) needs of some individuals, which can greatly influence the outcomes they achieve.

Multidisciplinary teams are not a new idea; indeed, they are recommended by NICE. It is hoped that our research will serve as part of a business case to, first, highlight how occupational therapy-led Enablement intervention can address the unique needs of autistic adults entering our service; second, prove the benefits of a timely multidisciplinary team working together under one roof to ensure autistic adults do not have to wait for specific interventions but have access to the right professionals at the right time before their situation becomes a crisis (often the point at which individuals require costly, specialist support in the long term); and third, and most important, provide a visual representation of how occupational therapy has drawn from theoretical frameworks that are forward thinking in relation to how we develop assessments to understand, and learn skills to support, autistic individuals with or without co-morbidities. We believe that without specialist Enablement intervention we will not be able to make a substantial difference to the lives of autistic people or reduce local authority costs in the long term. In short, the provision of timely support from a multidisciplinary team would mean that autistic individuals would be given a greater chance to achieve self-competence and independence at home and in the community.

Quality assurance: Links to SPELL

Thus far, we have analysed the degree to which we met our original research objectives and have proposed a baseline foundation for an ASC Enablement intervention. We feel we next need to quality assure the Kent Enablement intervention against established principles for best quality support for people on the autistic spectrum.

The goals of any autism intervention should be improved quality of life (Beadle-Brown 2017). Within our Enablement intervention we adhere to these key principles in this area:

- Understanding the nature of autism and its impact

- Reducing stress and anxiety

- Increasing adaptive behaviours

- Addressing problematic behaviours (to a lesser degree) by understanding the function of those behaviours and seeking to help mitigate them

These principles are very much in line with those of the National Autistic Society's (2001) SPELL framework:

Structure – We all need structure to plan our day and help predict events as best we can.

Positive approaches and expectations – Helping individuals in an individual way to achieve their potential.

Empathy – Supporting individuals to appreciate others' points of view and act upon this.

Low arousal – Supporting individuals to embrace good stress and reduce bad stress.

Links – Working with individuals, their supporters and partner agencies to provide consistent support and approaches.

Much of our Enablement work centres on helping people with *structure* because it is vital to improving opportunities and reducing anxiety. It is an area of strength for occupational therapists, particularly around helping clients to modify their environments and routines in order to improve their abilities, communication skills, relationships, choices, independence and so on. We spend a great deal of our time enabling individuals to structure their days, predict events and sequence elements of tasks. Another key element of our work is helping people to accept change and alterations to structure, promoting flexibility and transportation of ability across contexts.

Because Enablement is based on the goals set by the individual for themselves, we believe there has been a greater incentive to participate. This could not be a more *positive approach* in many ways. The clear majority of participants achieved their goals; however, if a goal seems completely beyond reach it is always worthwhile considering with an individual the part they can play in meeting it or whether a small element or even a variation of it is achievable. We believe we follow good practice in this area within specialist Enablement; that is, we assess skills, interests, roles and desired roles;

explore strengths and limitations; motivate in a sensitive, engaging and interactive way; use positive language and help to increase self-esteem; and really get to know the individual and what motivates them. Sometimes we experienced challenging situations; for example, we were encouraging a young person to adopt a more *positive* lifestyle, rich in social engagement and opportunity but the young person stated that they actually liked their life focused on their bedroom. This person told us that she was quite capable of deciding what she wanted in her own life. The solution we found was to be open and transparent and to develop a relationship of trust. From there we worked in partnership with her and supported her decision making as best we could while at the same times using the internet and social media to help her imagine what alternative lifestyles could be like.

Empathy in relation to people on the autistic spectrum is a subject often misunderstood. People on the spectrum can struggle to read others and their emotional states to varying degrees but to state that people with autism do not experience empathy for others is a complete myth. Sometimes a person might feel too much empathy regarding the situation of another or even an object, such as a book that never gets read. Rather, the empathetic processes of an autistic person are different to those of an average neurotypical person (see Baron-Cohen 2009). In the clients we support in the specialist Enablement intervention we clearly see theory of mind-type issues, but autism is a spectrum and, for that reason, people are affected to varying degrees by the traits of the condition. Some people are more able to empathise than others; some might utilise a superior intellect to learn strategies to compensate for difficulties in this area and try to say the right thing (ideally in the right context). We have used social skills programmes such as the National Autistic Society's SocialEyes to help in this area during the Enablement intervention, but the main starting point is assessment of the person's communication skills, learning style, experience of the world and sensory needs. It is necessary to understand the person to appreciate how they see the world and to respect their viewpoint, which may be different from that of others but not *wrong*. An additional point to acknowledge here is that neurotypical people can struggle to *read* an autistic person and consequently may not respond to them empathically.

A great deal of this book has discussed sensory integration and environmental/sensory impact. The fourth element of SPELL is *low arousal*, which refers to managing sensory stresses. The key issue here is that the ideal is certainly not *zero* stress/arousal but managed stress/arousal. We all need stress/arousal to function and be motivated to engage in activity and in terms of sensory need, in a clinical sense, some people need more than others. Important issues here – addressed within the specialist Enablement intervention – are applying communication approaches (context-specific communication) to help people improve focus and concentration; helping to create autistic-friendly environments, as free from distraction as possible; and supporting the rehearsal of unpleasant (to the individual) but unavoidable events – this needs to be managed very carefully so that it doesn't increase anxiety which might then become ritualistic (such as exposing someone to the object/subject of a phobia).

The specialist Enablement team rarely work in isolation and much of its success centres on making positive *links*. One of the key links – which we discuss later in this chapter – is the family carer, who is often as much a part of the Enablement process as the client, if the client so wishes. This is a sensible approach because if the person lives with their family, they will continue to be the main source of support when Enablement ends. For the Enablement outcomes to be sustained, all parties need to apply the approach consistently and understand and sign up to it, including family carers and future support services. The concept of links also covers helping the client to access opportunities available to them and, where necessary, providing support that is more specialised in terms of their needs. Though we do work with other agencies in supporting individuals' co-existing needs, often we needed services that were either not commissioned or hard to access, such as specialist ASC-adapted cognitive behavioural or sensory integration therapy. This is not a situation specific to Kent but is a global problem. In such cases we seek to meet the need as best we can through innovative support. The last point in this area is that, as part of our preventative Enablement intervention, for two years we also hosted a specialist information officer within the team, whose job it was to link clients to community resources and provide specialist information about autism. She developed a resources database for clients detailing services and sources of support which she had visited and checked were appropriate for people with autism (many services state that they are skilled in working with and accepting of people on the spectrum but the reality is sometimes different).

Recommendation   We recommend that our baseline foundation for intervention be utilised by other agencies to the benefit of their clients. We believe that our specialist Enablement intervention offers distinct possibilities for improving the quality of assessment and provision provided by autism teams. We present the Kent Enablement visual house as an outcome-based and measurable intervention; a key foundation for intervention that adheres to the principles of SPELL.

Further multidisciplinary support to complement occupational therapy in Enablement provision

As previously stated, NICE guidance calls for the establishment of 'autism teams'. Gillian Baird, chair of the guideline development group, stated that autism teams should provide 'key workers' to help people arrange support and interventions. It was advised that autism teams have a principal role in providing:

- Access to appropriate mainstream services

- Support for individuals and agencies across the pathway

- Access to local diagnostic assessment

- Post-diagnostic support

- Ongoing support for people with complex needs

- Liaison with health and social care staff

- Autism training to frontline staff

- Help for families and carers

Such teams could be integrated or virtual; if set up virtually, however, it is crucial that they 'join-up' in their overall delivery. We have only briefly mentioned the role of the social worker/case manager in specialist Enablement provision; in fact, during the Enablement research period each participant had an allocated social worker/key worker, that is, the social worker who originally assessed and referred them to the Enablement intervention. The social worker's role during the intervention was to deal with complex, time-intensive issues such as welfare benefits and (re)housing. Although the Enablement team helped in these areas in some cases, during the trial the enablers were a valuable and limited resource and they were best used in providing individualised, person-centred support. As we move on from offering Enablement as a trial intervention and instead a core provision of the team, we need to consider the nexus of the different roles within it.

Though we believe that occupational therapy approaches should be the basis for a community specialist ASC Enablement intervention, a logical question arises regarding whether the approach could be improved in its overall outcomes by greater multidisciplinary input – not just within Enablement itself but in some cases pre-Enablement, preparing for Enablement. We encounter a small number of potential Enablement clients with such ingrained psychological issues that they are not yet ready to tackle the basement level of development. This is because they cannot adequately engage in and focus upon the assessment, let alone the interventions; they need a specialist health intervention first. One client in the Enablement cohort was affected significantly in this way – it would have been great if we could have accessed specialist MDT support for him, internally or virtually, in a timely manner to meet his wider needs, emotional and psychological. A question remains regarding whether occupational therapy and psychological interventions could occur simultaneously during an Enablement intervention period. It may be that this is too much for one person to manage.

Below we describe the roles we feel are needed in an autism team to support people in making optimum and sustained long-term progress, within and beyond the Enablement provision.

Psychologist

We believe that Enablement interventions provided in a timely manner across the lifespan will help to reduce the need for psychological interventions. However, the psychological needs of some participants – one or two in our cohort – impacted upon their ability to engage with the Enablement support. It would have been beneficial to have had internal psychological support as a foundation for Enablement, to improve participants' focus, motivation and overall well-being. Most importantly, psychological input could add great value to an integrated health and social care assessment for those who require it. This is one of the true benefits of a multidisciplinary team: it can provide complementary layers of assessment to enable a comprehensive understanding of the person. Psychological input could also support the planning and facilitation of psycho-educational groups or one-to-one therapy. A psychologist's 'understanding that challenging behaviour develops to serve important functions for people' (Gore *et al.* 2013) would help the team as a whole develop strategies for both the client and ourselves to manage such.

Speech and language therapist

We agree with www.researchautism.com (2014) that speech and language therapy (SLT) 'may help some individuals on the autism spectrum, especially when it is provided as one element of a combined, multi-component programme delivered by a multi-disciplinary team, and when that multi-component programme is personalised to the needs of the individual'. A vast array of communication difficulties exists – we have met people on the spectrum who are electively mute, who have developed foreign accents as a result of copying actors on the television, and who have very good verbal abilities but struggle to transfer their skills across different contexts (that is, understanding that people generally express themselves differently at school, at home and in a bar, for example). The work of speech and language therapists (SLTs) can also produce health benefits because they can provide treatment and support for children and adults who have difficulties with eating, drinking and swallowing. SLTs can also help with conditions such as dyslexia, dysphasia and apraxia, which may also impact upon individuals on the spectrum. They can advise on communication aids and alternative tools of communication and also help people see the *value* of communication. The Enablement Spectrum Star™ measurements (see Table 5.1) show that social skills and communication outcomes displayed slightly lower success rates than other areas and could potentially have been improved if SLTs had been part of the Enablement team.

Table 5.1 Spectrum Star™ completed measurements (weeks 1 to 24) for communication and social skills

Domain area	Week 1 score	Week 12 score	Difference between week 1 and 12
Communication	5.52	6.74	1.22
Social skills	4.61	6.22	1.61

Specialist community nurse

An ASC community nurse in the Enablement team would address clients' health needs and also help with co-existing health conditions if necessary. A person's independence and well-being can be severely impacted by a health condition, such as epilepsy. Sometimes a person's autism will be a factor impacting their ability to self-manage the co-existing condition; for example, and to use epilepsy again, we have met clients who were capable of managing their epileptic medication but struggled to balance dosages in relation to dietary intake or became fixed on professional advice given once in a certain context but not relevant to all contexts. A specialist community nurse could also help clients with strategies to manage harmful (to themselves or others) behaviour, including weight issues. Table 5.2 shows the Spectrum Star™ outcome measurements for physical health, socially responsible behaviour and relationships, revealing that greater success may have been possible if a specialist community nurse had been part of the Enablement team – socially responsible behaviour and relationships demonstrating the least change.

Table 5.2 Spectrum Star™ completed measurements (weeks 1 to 24) for relationships, socially responsible behaviour and physical health

Domain area	Week 1 score	Week 12 score	Difference between week 1 and 12
Relationships	5.52	6.22	0.70
Socially responsible behaviour	8.04	8.57	0.53
Physical health	5.39	6.74	1.35

Whilst discussing the additional roles that would benefit specialist Enablement intervention, it is probably reasonable to question whether Enablement interventions would assist people with all neurodevelopmental issues and not just autism. Indeed, a suggestion has been made (supported by Judith Gould, lead consultant at the NAS Lorna Wing Centre for Autism, who reviewed this book) that a 'neurodevelopmental team' is ideal, rather than a stand-alone 'ASC team', because issues with other neurodevelopmental conditions cannot always be seen as separate from an ASC. These other neurodevelopmental conditions are often misunderstood and inadequately supported, which is not a criticism of professionals working in this area because it is very complex and conditions and syndromes can mimic each other. For example, a person who is 'constantly mulling over anxieties can look distracted, and this behaviour can be confused with ADHD' (Kutscher 2005, p. 16). The solution must surely be to provide a functional assessment focused on the individual, carried out by a neurodevelopmental multidisciplinary team?

Recommendation   Improved outcome-fulfilment for the client and cost-effectiveness for the authority would result from creating multidisciplinary Enablement teams. We believe that Enablement interventions, in general, would be improved through specialist professional input. We also believe that specialist Enablement should be a neurodevelopmental rather than autism-specific intervention.

Impact of co-existing conditions

One group of Enablement participants harder to engage with in real terms were participants whose autism was over-shadowed and impacted upon by another primary co-existing condition, such as unstable mental health or unmedicated ADHD. These conditions often result in a lack of focus and attention on tasks and goals. This cohort should be differentiated from clients who have a range of co-existing conditions in which autism might well be the primary issue but 'shadow syndromes' also exist (Ratey and Johnson 1998) that need to be acknowledged but may not necessarily affect the impact of an ASC Enablement intervention. Where these shadow syndromes are neurodevelopmental in nature, there is every possibility that specialist Enablement can help. Indeed, the Enablement research revealed that, for participants with autism and co-existing ADHD, exceptional cost reductions were made – a £184.59 average weekly saving per person – although for an admittedly small cohort of just five clients. In comparison, for participants with autism and co-existing diagnosed metal health issues, a less significant cost saving was made; in fact, a third of that of the average reduction (£60.92 per person over six clients) found for those with co-existing ADHD. If this trend continues it poses a question regarding how best to support clients with co-existing mental health issues and an ASC.

In one case, Enablement, by virtue of its intensive interaction and involvement with an individual, identified a level of co-existing need which was not previously understood and may not have been identified at a one-off assessment. Here, the Enablement team was able to use the details of their specialist assessment to make onward referrals to health providers to address the co-existing need.

Recommendation   Early indications (within a small sample group) indicate that clients with overall neurodevelopmental issues benefit significantly from the Enablement intervention. Early indications also suggest that clients impacted by unstable mental health or unmedicated ADHD are less likely to benefit – two areas which appeared in the list of key reasons for withdrawing from Enablement early. To clarify this statement more fully, unlike for autism in its purest sense, medication can help those severely affected by ADHD to better manage living with their condition and to be better able to focus on personal development. This leads us to two recommendations: first, for further analysis of this area as more clients are offered an Enablement intervention, and, second, for providers to establish a *screening process* or *eligibility criteria* because an Enablement provision over 12 weeks, especially if multidisciplinary, is clearly a valuable resource – an opportunity that needs to be allocated to the people most likely to benefit from and engage with it.

This leads neatly into our next area of key learning.

Readiness for change

Separate from the formal research measurements and analysis, the practitioners providing the Enablement intervention stated anecdotally that they struggled most with participants who were *encouraged* to participate but in retrospect had not totally committed to engaging with the provision; a small number of participants, it was felt, agreed to Enablement to please others. There are a number of associated factors here: some people may have actually wanted to participate in Enablement and found it too demanding – they might not have been able to imagine what Enablement would be like and the overall demands made upon them; some people may have wanted to participate and then experienced changes in their life (for example, many of the participants had issues with housing during the Enablement period); or they might have agreed initially because they felt pressured to do so by an external authority. Whatever the reason, and many are valid, it is important for an Enablement provider to ensure that the person is ready to embark upon a journey of change and is willing to engage fully, even if participation might at times come at personal cost, that is, because any change for a person on the spectrum can be unsettling.

Recommendation   As stated previously, a robust screening process or eligibility criteria is needed to ensure that those most likely to benefit can access such a resource-limited service. One approach to ensuring engagement might be for those who have benefitted from the intervention to describe the experience to others – *in person* or through social media. There is no better advocate of a product than people who have successfully used it. In an ideal world people on the spectrum who have been through Enablement could work as enablers for others.

Enablement as a person-centred holistic approach

One element of the Kent specialist Enablement provision concerned an area that was somewhat of a *gamble*, a leap of faith. Most Enablement interventions – with their dual aims of improving autonomy and outcomes and simultaneously reducing long-term dependency and associated costs – designate goals for an individual that are centred on those activities which 'cost' money to support. An example is a person with a learning or physical disability who has a *costed* package of support to help them cook a meal – they would be designated Enablement to enable them to cook a meal independently. In contrast, within our Enablement intervention, the client chooses the goal they wanted to work on – of course, we had completed specialist assessments, including the Spectrum Star™, which may have provided a level of professional *lead* towards a particular goal, but we were not insistent that the participant worked on the lowest-scoring area or a specific task. The reason this approach may be seen as a gamble is that we could have helped a participant to achieve a 'goal' but not reduced the cost of their care package. For the research sample, the evidence suggests that overall we achieved both aims: fulfilment of personal goals/outcomes and a reduction in costed packages of care. We believe we achieved this because our holistic approach is entirely person-centred. By utilising the bottom-up approach, we enabled the individual to not only achieve a specific goal but also increase core functional ability; the result is that the person can better transfer that ability across other goals and contexts. Below are some elements of our person-centred, context-specific approach:

- Using personal and identifiable objects in visual prompts such as a client's own oven rather than a picture of an oven.

- Using pictures of actual landmarks on a bus journey when planning travel training.

- Using technical supports for time and activity issues, such as apps or Abilia's MEMOdayplanner, which breaks down the day into 15-minute chunks and counts down to that activity.

- Learning social skills in the right contextual environment – as Vermeulen (2012) states, a conversation in a dentist's waiting room might be different to that with friends. We also used parts of the National Autistic Society's SocialEyes programme but individualised it to suit people's actual contexts.

- Ensuring social stories were based upon real situations and real people known to the person.

As Enablement progresses in Kent, we continue to explore person-centred solutions to meet people's needs, in whichever way suits the individual. Currently, we are trialling 'zones of regulation' (Kuypers 2011) and interoception approaches (Mahler 2016) through practical solutions for improving self-regulation, self awareness and social understanding. We also continue to trial various forms of technology.

Recommendation We recommend gaining a holistic picture of the individual, including learning style and ability, sensory preferences, familiar elements of their environment and the context within which they live. An intervention based on this information is more likely to result in the individual achieving their goals; additionally, they will be better able to transfer what they have learnt to other contexts and other goals/outcomes. If they are able to choose their own goals/outcomes, the individual appears to be more motivated to engage.

Post-Enablement learning

We predicted, from the Spectrum Star™, a slight overall regression in participants' measurements between weeks 12 and 24 because a highly intensive and personalised service is unlikely to end without some form of consequence; unfortunately, Enablement has to be time-limited. This is a situation akin to a student leaving a specialist school and regressing when the skilled support and structured engagement end. In both scenarios there needs to be a robust onward plan if the person has ongoing needs. The majority of our participants (of those who did not finish early) required some ongoing support, but for far fewer hours (see Table 5.3).

Table 5.3 Evidence of ongoing support

Size of package – by hours	Week 1	Week 24
Clients with no package	0	11
Clients with package of 6 or fewer hours per week (approx. £70 per week)	7	14
Clients with package of over 6 hours	25	7

We were very pleased to find that some clients felt that they did not need ongoing support post-Enablement, and though the majority did need ongoing support it was at reduced levels. These results differ from those expected of other client groups post-Enablement, for whom it is envisaged that a large percentage would require no ongoing need for care and support; for example, a person leaving hospital, enabled as they recover from an injury. The difference in ASC Enablement is that we are providing a service to people on the spectrum who are *most in need*, those with a more complex presentation of a lifelong condition; if they had a very low level of need, they would not have been assessed for a support package or referred to adult services in the first place; indeed, we currently provide a package of support to only 20 per cent of all those referred.

Interestingly, for our research cohort there was a further cost saving in terms of care and support packages between weeks 12 and 24 – amounting to £35,098.44 per year overall. There may be back stories to explain some of these reductions, but clearly Enablement contributed to this additional decrease. As regards the Spectrum

Star™ results for weeks 12 to 24, a small regression was evident; the areas that were self-assessed to be most affected were Living skills and self-care, Sensory differences, Physical health, Socially responsible behaviour and Relationships – all by one point or less. But when considered over the whole 24 weeks every area evidenced improvements, on average; in the areas of Living skills and self-care and Sensory differences, participants, on average, progressed 2 points overall over the 24 weeks – a marked and significant *journey of change*.

Thus far we have discussed post-assessment measurements and costs, but there is an equally significant finding post-Enablement: for clients with longer-term need we often require specialist community support services to take on the personalised ongoing plan and strategy; services that are few and far between. Though we do have some good services, there are not enough – a situation in no way unique to autism; in terms of community care support in the UK, demand is currently greater than supply (Skills for Care 2016), and particularly so in specialist areas.

Understanding of autism, even in social and health care arenas, remains significantly underdeveloped, and high-quality ASC resources are scarce. The providers who have successfully taken forward and sustained our Enablement interventions are mostly those charging higher prices because they offer more specialist support for people with neurodevelopmental issues and invest in associated training. A case example of good quality sustainable post-Enablement support concerned a man for whom the intervention uncovered a specialist health need. Despite his complex need, Enablement still helped him to venture out of his house and engage in positive activity (only his family had been able to encourage him to do so in recent years). Post-Enablement, the specialist provider commissioned to supply ongoing support fed-back that the client had shared a laugh with the support worker for the first time and also recalled to his mother details of his day – two major advancements relative to this client's overall difficulties. The provider understood the Enablement intervention and also the wider principles of active and positive support and was able to take on the agreed post-Enablement tasks. This is a rare example; not all of our Enablement participants with longer-term need receive sufficient high-quality support (in our opinion) because they are referred to generic community providers, with little to moderate understanding of autism.

There are, of course, other long-term solutions to meeting ongoing 'need', which do not always involve formal care and support services. One of the best solutions is to help the person gain substantial meaningful activity such as work, because, drawing on an observation of Vermeulen's – work can be the panacea of all things. Work does not have to be full time: it can refer to an apprenticeship, work experience, a voluntary position or a part-time position boosted by tax credits. Part-time work is often desirable for our client group because some people on the spectrum struggle with consecutive days of social engagement; one man described the situation as his battery gradually draining – as he worked hard to fit in at work, he then needed time to recharge the battery. Any meaningful structured activity will help a person on the spectrum; however, it does not necessarily have to be work-related. An activity that provides predictability and routine; companionship and socialisation; motivation, role enhancement and status, and so on, can make a huge difference to an autistic person's life. Just being in shared spaces and meeting common goals with others quickly become part of the person's support structure, and can very much compensate for the loss of intensive Enablement support.

If work is not within reach and the person does not have a private income, they will need welfare benefits to sustain themselves. Specialist Enablement has been able to help in this area by providing specific reports on individuals pertaining to what they can and cannot do. Welfare agencies tend to make judgements based on the recommendations of such reports; that is, they provide the appropriate benefit. It is hard to argue with a thorough specialist assessment based on evidenced personal capabilities.

Recommendation An Enablement intervention should be designed and facilitated together with a forward plan detailing how longer-term ASC support can be provided for those who need it. There may be a case for higher levels of funding for specialist community support services. People who have been assessed as eligible for support and then been supported by Specialist Enablement, resulting in a recommendation for reduced but longer-term specialist support, must surely have a case to argue for a higher premium of targeted specialist support?

We continue to work on stimulating the market to encourage skilled care and support providers to respond to the recommendations of Enablement interventions, but another option in terms of sustaining a person who needs formal support would be to use Personal assistants (PAs) who are knowledgeable in the field of autism. Since the introduction of the Direct Payment system in 1997, individuals have been able to opt for a personal budget to pay for and source their own care. Many local authorities assist this process by holding a database of PAs looking for support hours. Specialist PAs would benefit from membership of a peers' support network because the role can be challenging and they might not otherwise realise opportunities to engage with work colleagues.

Recognising the value of qualitative assessment

Of all the Enablement research measurements, the assessment tools which proved most useful within this study were the Spectrum Star™ and the participant exit questionnaire. This is not to discount the quantitative cost measurements – a principal consideration for budget holders – but the real value of the approach was validated by the self-assessed qualitative measurements. As a local authority provider we must always supply transparent and qualitative performance data, and canvassing client opinion is arguably the most constructive approach to gathering such.

Although some participants needed time to understand the scoring system and descriptors of the Spectrum Star™, this tool provided a fuller more-personalised assessment than any standard Care Act 2104 template; standard social care assessments may link to outcomes but rarely provide measurements to review progress to the extent possible using the Spectrum Star™. Scores are not a qualitative measure, clearly, but they can be used as the basis for a discussion about the quality of provision and for informing decisions made about the outcomes an individual wants to achieve. As stated previously, however, an Enablement participant is quite at liberty to choose an outcome which does not link naturally to their score ratings; it is totally within their gift.

The exit questionnaire meanwhile was very much centred on the *lived* experience of the participant, and provided valuable feedback. Essentially, at week 12 we *know* the person, having worked intensively with them – sometimes hand on hand – we have witnessed what they can and cannot do, and helped to mitigate their difficulties and enhance their skills wherever we could.

Recommendation If other agencies are considering adopting the Kent Enablement intervention, we recommend that they utilise the Spectrum Star™ and exit questionnaire as their principal qualitative measurements (together with a quantitative cost analysis measurement). For the Kent ASC Team, the

Spectrum Star™ has proven to be the most useful self-assessment instrument for eliciting person-centred goals and outcomes.

Using the research results to inform the delivery of other services

Autism is a lifelong condition, so it is not surprising that, for many people on the spectrum, the honing of skills through Enablement intervention is needed for more than the short term and may even be necessary across the lifespan. This was a point made strongly by the members of the Enablement Research Focus Group – a collaborative steering group comprising clients, carers and providers and those working in education, health and academia – who felt that people newly diagnosed at whatever age should be seen as those who would benefit from an initial Enablement intervention, and possible follow-up interventions during periods of change, such as transition. It is not only the timing of an Enablement intervention that is significant, however. We also believe that Enablement interventions could be successful adopted in other contexts and settings to those discussed here; that is, beyond the home/community setting. We feel that our adult-based research could benefit wider service delivery within the areas discussed below.

Children's health and social care

Children's health and social care services could use the Enablement intervention to support autistic clients, plus their parents and siblings. Core local authority provisions for disabled children and their families, such as that in Kent, increase in breadth all the time. Services offer paediatric support, educational/school nursing and educational psychology support, children's and adolescents' mental health services, groups and hubs, carers' and parents' groups, early help to prevent increased need and support the family, and the National Autistic Society's EarlyBird and Cygnet programmes, to name just a few. Despite this significant offer, the overall provision for children and families can still be improved further we feel, because some of the more specialist interventions are not always available to those without a learning disability but nonetheless still struggling at home with autism. It would make sense to consider using the Kent Enablement intervention within support provided to children and their families: to assist children in their development and opportunities for personal fulfilment and to seek to reduce the complexity of their needs as they approach adulthood; and also to help parents (some of which might also have autism). A parent of a young adult with autism who assisted our Enablement Research Focus Group summed up her thoughts regarding the provision of Enablement in childhood thus:

> As a parent of a young person with autism, I would agree strongly that starting Enablement earlier is preferable. These are the sorts of skills that parents are particularly anxious for their offspring to gain, because their independence as adults is so reliant on having these skills. And the later Enablement starts, the more 'undoing' of established habits may have to take place.

A further area in which earlier Enablement intervention could help is *sleep*. Three Enablement research participants made significant improvements in the quality of their sleep following our intervention, a goal that had eluded them for most of their lives. A child of 'higher' ability on the autistic spectrum, such as these three had been, had probably not been offered a sleep assessment or given the opportunity to develop a 'sundowners' routine (which could include relaxation techniques and/or avoidance of stimulants such as tea or alcohol or backlit computer screens), or to undertake a sensory assessment to see if equipment or weighted therapy could help. How much better would their life chances have been if they had received such specialist support in earlier life?

Employment

Many disabled people struggle to gain employment, as borne out by the statistics: 93 per cent of people with moderate to severe learning disabilities are unemployed – this percentage includes many people with autism (Kent County Council 2017); only 16 per cent of autistic adults are in full-time paid employment; and only 32 per cent are in some kind of paid work (National Autistic Society 2016). Many struggle to hold down a job or keep moving to new jobs. We can see only benefits accruing from Enablement interventions in this area because the whole approach centres on maximising potential in environmental and occupational contexts. The vocational profiles of clients with autism who are being supported to find employment should be augmented by occupational therapy Enablement assessment tools.

Shared Lives

Shared Lives is a fostering scheme for adults with a disability. Host families open their homes to clients who might otherwise be living in a more restricted environment, such as residential care, as a result of complex needs. We believe that an excellent expansion of our intervention would be to provide Enablement in a Shared Lives setting. In this way the Enablement team would not only be supporting the individual but also coaching the host family. After a period, the team would cease working with them and then the host family would continue the Enablement support. Ideally, the Enablement team would be virtually available to help with any queries or struggles along the way. Though the scheme can provide a long-term home, this does not have to be the case for everyone; such a nexus of support would be ideal as short- to medium-term provision for a young adult, possibly leaving state care as a child. After a period it would be hoped that the individual could secure their own tenancy.

Reintegration into the community

Dealing with change can be a significant challenge for an autistic individual and no more so than if that person is being discharged from prison or leaving a secure mental health hospital to return to the community. We know that a disproportionate number of people with an ASC come to the attention of the criminal justice system, and an even higher number of people with ADHD (Brewer and Young 2015). Mental health facilities in every health commissioning area in the UK will have patients with autism; however, there is a severe lack of specialist support to help them reintegrate into the community. Offering individuals leaving such highly structured and restrictive environments the immediate support of a specialist multidisciplinary Enablement team can only be beneficial, we feel. People may actually be diagnosed with autism while in such environments, particularly prison. We have met clients in prison who have been provided with behavioural support and anger management but have never been assessed effectively to ascertain the underlying cause of such issues. An assessment followed by appropriate support may reduce the likelihood of a return to these environments.

Recommendation We suggest that opportunities to use the specialist Enablement intervention in other services be explored, including commissioned support services, work with autistic children and parents, within education, and for people leaving institutional settings such as prison and mental health units.

Carers' support and involvement in specialist Enablement

During our Specialist Enablement research period it became obvious that we had underestimated carers' needs when planning for intervention. The majority of carers we met were highly supportive of the intervention and wanted the 'cared for' to do well; however, we had not envisaged how much more time we needed to work in partnership with some carers. As many of the research team were themselves carers of adult children with autism and other neurodevelopmental conditions, we fully understood how hard it can be to 'let go'. A small number of carers were exhausted by their situation and wanted us to get on with the work without too much involvement from them. Many wanted us to listen to them and their concerns as they did not or could not access support for themselves. Where agreeable, case managers offered them a carers' assessment under the Care Act 2014. This Act affords the same status to clients and carers and we sought to address the needs of both. Responses to our Carers' Questionnaire illustrated the lack of support available to carers of autistic adults beyond advice and guidance. We return to this issue later in this chapter.

Where the person lives at home, working with their family is crucial to the success of the Enablement intervention. This is also the case where family carers provide substantial support to the person in their own home. Greater time and attention needs to be allocated to family carers and they need to be supported in a sensitive manner; the support nexus will not be successful if the professional goes in thinking they know best and do not work in partnership. Professionals are in that person's life for very short periods of time; family carers are often there on a permanent basis.

Recommendation   Carers' needs must also be taken into account. The establishment of an online carers' support group might be beneficial as might a peer support system.

Need for further research

The research contributes to the evidence base regarding the role of occupational therapy within an intervention for individuals with autism. It demonstrates the benefits of using an approach that focuses on modifying and adapting activities and context. It indicates positive outcomes for 30 recipients of a specialist Enablement intervention using a person-centred approach in which participants chose the goals they wanted to achieve in settings of their choice and which took their preferred learning style into account. Pre- and post-assessments and evaluations were not undertaken by the individuals delivering specialist Enablement, which reduced desirability bias and made research results more reliable and valid. Validity of the results was strengthened by application of the participant exit questionnaire, but could have been further strengthened by more input from carers, as well as neutral observers carrying out pre- and post- assessments rather than those who selected participants for specialist intervention. The *generalisability* of our results is unclear because we did not measure whether research findings could be applied to other settings and the sample was relatively small; participants were drawn from clients using adult social services. The issues discussed indicate the need for further research with a larger sample size; exploration of whether improvements can be transferred to other contexts; and the incorporation of follow-up assessment data gained three months post-intervention (to measure maintenance of any improvements).

The research results did pose some questions that may warrant further research:

1) Does early sensory work have the potential to sustain functional improvements for autistic people of all ages over time?

2) Do older clients gain more benefit from specialist Enablement intervention; are they more committed; are they emotionally more resilient and hence less anxious about the intervention coming to an end; are they better at sustaining improvements in the learnt skills?

3) Is intervention of more benefit to those living independently?

4) Do carers have a role to play in whether an intervention is successful or not?

5) Is further exploration of the needs of parents/carers across the lifespan warranted?

6) Is there a link between females in general being diagnosed later and their more positive experience of specialist Enablement as a means of increasing independence? Are females more realistic regarding the goals of independence?

7) Does improvement in functional skills in one area of daily living also lead to improvements in other areas, for example well-being?

8) Does a more intensive multi-disciplinary provision of specialist ASC Enablement yield greater cost savings/avoidance?

Final comments

Enablement, as provided in adult services, is aimed at improving autonomy and outcomes whilst reducing long-term dependency and costs. Specialist ASC Enablement seeks to address the gaps in conventional occupational therapist-led adult Enablement that result in limitations to address the specialist needs of people on the autistic spectrum. These needs require a specialist focus on sensory, social, motor-processing and adaptive interaction. Specialist Enablement is also grounded in a person-centred approach, with individuals choosing the goals they want to achieve rather than being expected to fit in a schedule determined by professionals.

Kent County Council's research has wielded a plethora of data which demonstrates that specialist Enablement could facilitate positive change allowing for the self-management of high-functioning autistic people living in the community. We believe that this has been achieved as a result of the holistic, person-centred approach adopted by the specialist Enablement team. It utilised a bottom-up approach which enabled the individual to not just meet a specific goal but also increase core functional ability; the result of this approach was an improved ability to transfer skills to other goals and contexts.

Key recommendations had a strategic as well as service-specific dimension. Strategic recommendations are to continue using the specialist Enablement approach in the Kent ASC Team; to seek to include a core offer of Enablement in the newly designed ASC Team; and to explore opportunities for specialist Enablement to be used in other services, for example commissioned support services. Service-specific recommendations are to enhance the delivery of specialist Enablement through multidisciplinary input in the ASC Team; to consider how best we work with carers in future and how we help meet their needs for more support; to have clear eligibility criteria and to apply robust screening of applicants for specialist Enablement; to facilitate the provision of peer support and learning/mentoring from those who have undergone Enablement to others new to the service.

Overall, we hope that this book offers readers a greater insight into some of the difficulties experienced by autistic people. We have demonstrated how our bottom-up framework has been useful in guiding our assessments, interventions and evaluations as we seek to help autistic adults achieve greater levels of independence. The framework is also useful for identifying gaps in our knowledge and the service. We believe that the outcomes achieved by participants during the Enablement intervention are more important than the resultant cost savings (or cost avoidance). These include clients sleeping well for the first time in years, no longer feeling suicidal, finding employment, using public transport, reducing medication, cooking independently, gaining a better understanding of how to communicate with others – the list goes on. Many of our clients have experienced a life-altering journey of change.

The cost savings/avoidance associated with supporting individuals on the spectrum in terms of self-management and well-being are almost impossible to equate because they are experienced within so many different settings and agencies. A person on the spectrum employed or otherwise in positive, productive occupation could reasonably be assumed to have better mental/emotional health and to be less reliant on the benefit system, the health system, the prison service and so on.

This is the greatest thing we have learnt: that despite a lack of *new* money in this time of economic austerity, and as such no new funding for 'autism', a great deal of money is nonetheless spent on supporting those with an ASC. These costs are hidden within residential care, mental health services, the criminal justice system and the benefit system – along with many other settings. These are the very funds which could be partly redirected to support community-based multidisciplinary autism teams across the lifespan; to provide preventative, bottom-up approaches, such as Enablement, to help people on the spectrum so that they *do not need* those reactive, high-cost interventions.

It is hoped that other authorities and services that provide assessment and support for all autistic individuals, whatever their age, will utilise our finding and framework as a way forward in procuring the services of those professionals fundamental to their teams. We propose the adoption of a consistent approach throughout the UK so that autistic people can access intervention at the right time in their lives – be it at diagnosis or during periods of transition – wherever they live, because we believe this will not only result in local authority savings and prevent the need for high-cost packages of support but also give autistic people the chance to achieve their full potential.

Bibliography

Attwood, T. (2004) 'Diagnosis of Asperger syndrome.' Accessed on 04/05/2017 at www.reboundtherapy.org/papers/aspergers/diagnosis_of_aspergers_by_tony_attwood.

Autism Speaks (2014) 'Lifetime costs of autism average $1.4 million to $2.4 million.' Accessed on 04/05/2017 at www.autismspeaks.org/science/science-news/lifetime-costs-autism-average-millions.

Ayres, J. (1979) *Sensory Integration and the Child.* Torrance, CA: Western Psychological Services.

Baron-Cohen, S. (2009) 'Autism: The empathizing–systemizing (E–S) theory.' *Annals of the New York Academy of Sciences* 1156, 68–80.

Baron-Cohen, S., Leslie, A., and Frith, U. (1985) 'Does the autistic child have a theory of mind?' *Cognition* 21, 1, 37–46.

Beadle-Brown, J. (2017) 'Supporting children and adults on the autistic spectrum.' Presentation for Kent County Council, Canterbury.

Brewer, N. and Young, R. (2015) *Crime and Autism Spectrum Disorder.* London: Jessica Kingsley Publishers.

Brown, C. and Dunn, W. (2002) *Adolescent/Adult Sensory Profile.* San Antonio, TX: PsychCorp.

Burns, S. and MacKeith, J. (2012) *Spectrum Star*™. Triangle Consulting Social Enterprise Ltd. Accessed on 06/08/2017 at www.outcomestar.org.uk.

Duncan, E. (2006) 'The model of human occupation: Integrating theory into practice.' In E. Duncan (ed.) *Foundations for Practice in Occupational Therapy*, 4th edition. London: Elsevier.

Erikson, E. (1950) *Childhood and Society*. New York: W. W. Norton and Co.

Fisher, A. and Bray Jones, K. (2010) *Assessment of Motor and Process Skills*. Volume 1: *Development, Standardization, and Administration Manual*, 7th edition. Fort Collins, CO: Three Star Press.

Frith, C. and Frith, U. (2008) 'Implicit and explicit processes in social cognition.' *Neuron* 60, 3, 503–510.

Gore, N., McGill, P., Toogood, S., Allen, D. *et al.* (2013) 'Definition and scope for positive behavioural support.' *International Journal of Positive Behavioural Support* 3, 2.

Grandin, T. (2006) *Thinking in Pictures: My Life with Autism*. New York: Vintage.

Kent County Council (2017) *Working Together, Improving Outcomes: Kent's Strategy for Children and Young People with Special Educational Needs and Disabilities, 2017–2019*. Accessed on 05/08/2017 at https://democracy.kent.gov.uk/documents/s76228/Item%20B5%20SEND%20Strategy.pdf.

Kutscher, M. (2005) *Kids in the Syndrome Mix*. London: Jessica Kingsley Publishers.

Kuypers, L. (2011) *The Zones of Regulation*. San Jose, CA: Think Social Publishing.

Mahler, K. (2016). Interoception: *The Eighth Sensory System: Practical Solutions for Improving Self-Regulation, Self-Awareness and Social Understanding of Individuals With Autism Spectrum and Related Disorders*. Shawnee Mission, KS: AAPC Publishing.

Mills, R. and Kenyon, S. (2013) 'Prevalence study of females with autism in the four participating countries.' Accessed on 11/05/2017 at http://autisminpink.net.

Mucklow, N. (2009) *The Sensory Team Handbook: A Hands-on Tool to Help Young People Make Sense of Their Senses and Take Charge of Their Sensory Processing*, 2nd edition (p. 16). Ontario, Canada: Michael Grass House.

National Audit Office (2009) 'Supporting people with autism through adulthood.' Accessed on 05/08/2017 at www.nao.org.uk/report/supporting-people-with-autism-through-adulthood.

National Autistic Society (2001) 'SPELL framework.' Accessed on 04/05/2017 at www.autism.org.uk/about/strategies/spell.aspx.

National Autistic Society (2016) 'The autism employment gap: Too much information in the workplace.' Accessed on 06/08/2017 at www.db.com/newsroom_news/TMI_Employment_Report_24pp_WEB.pdf.

Newman, B. and Newman, P. (2015) *Development through Life: A Psychosocial Approach*, 12th edition. Stamford, CA: Cengage Learning.

NICE (2014) 'Implementing NICE guidance on autism: Developing autism teams.' Accessed on 06/08/2017 at www.nice.org.uk.

Ratey, J. and Johnson, C. (1998) *Shadow Syndromes: The Mild Forms of Mental Disorder which Sabotage Us*. New York: Bantam Books.

Skills for Care (2016) 'The state of the adult social care sector and workforce in England.' Accessed on 06/08/2017 at www.skillsforcare.org.uk.

Vermeulen, P. (2012) *Autism as Context Blindness*. Kansas City, KS: AAPC Publishing.

Werling, D. and Geschwind, D. (2015) 'Sex difference in autistic spectrum conditions.' Accessed on 02/05/2017 at www.ncbi.nlm.nih.gov/pmc/articles/PMC4164392.

Willey, L. (1999) *Pretending to be Normal*. London: Jessica Kingsley Publishers.

Williams, M. and Shellenberger, S. (1996) *How Does Your Engine Run?® A Leader's Guide to the Alert Program for Self-regulation*. Albuquerque, NM: Therapy Works, Inc.

Index